PIANO · VOCAL · GUITAR

ETERNAL GLORY

Songs for Memorial Services

ISBN 0-634-03010-8

HAL•LEONARD®
CORPORATION
7777 W. BLUEMOUND RD. P.O. BOX 13819 MILWAUKEE, WI 53213

Visit Hal Leonard Online at
www.halleonard.com

4	Abide with Me
6	Amazing Grace
12	Ave Maria (Schubert)
16	Beautiful Isle of Somewhere
9	Because He Lives
18	Blessed Assurance
20	Deep River
22	Does Jesus Care?
24	For All the Saints
27	Friends
32	Give Me Jesus
34	He Shall Feed His Flock
40	He the Pearly Gates Will Open
42	His Eye Is on the Sparrow
44	Home Free
37	How Great Thou Art
52	I Walked Today Where Jesus Walked
58	I'll Fly Away
60	If You Could See Me Now
70	In the Garden
72	It Is Well with My Soul
67	Ivory Palaces
74	Jesus Will Still Be There
78	Just a Closer Walk with Thee
80	The Lord's Prayer
84	My Savior First of All
86	O That Will Be Glory
88	On Jordan's Stormy Banks
90	Panis Angelicus (O Lord Most Holy)
94	Peace in the Valley
96	Precious Lord, Take My Hand
98	Rock of Ages
102	Sweet By and By
104	Swing Low, Sweet Chariot
99	Tears Are a Language
106	Then Shall the Righteous Shine
110	The Twenty-Third Psalm
116	We'll Understand It Better By and By
118	What a Friend We Have in Jesus
120	When I Lay My Burden Down
122	When We All Get to Heaven
124	You'll Never Walk Alone

ABIDE WITH ME

Words by HENRY F. LYTE
Music by WILLIAM H. MONK

A - bide with me. Fast falls the e - ven - tide.
I need Thy pre - sence ev - 'ry pass - ing hour.

The dark - ness deep - ens, Lord, with me a - bide.
What but thy grace can foil the tempt - er's pow'r?

When oth - er help - ers fail and com - forts flee,
Who, like Thy - self, my guide and stay can be?

Help of the
Through cloud and

AMAZING GRACE

Words by JOHN NEWTON
Traditional American Melody

Moderately

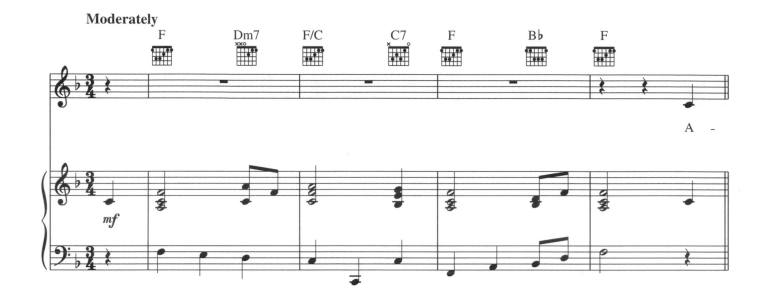

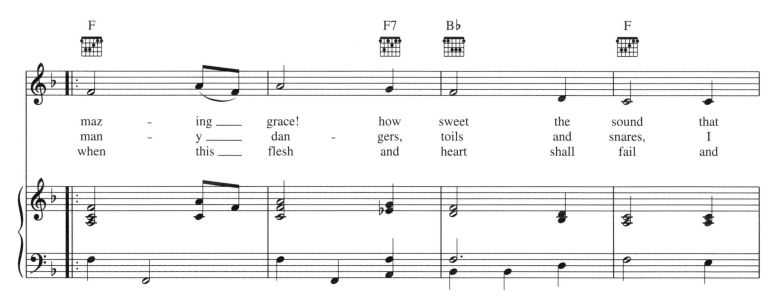

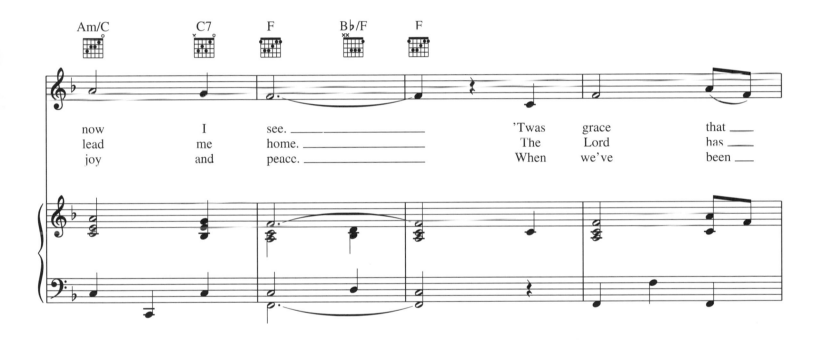

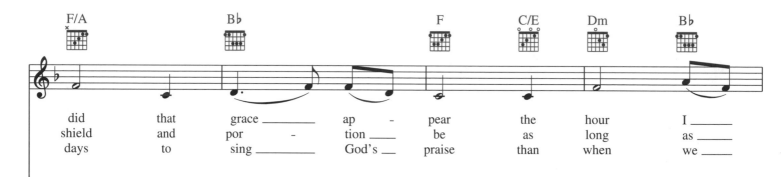

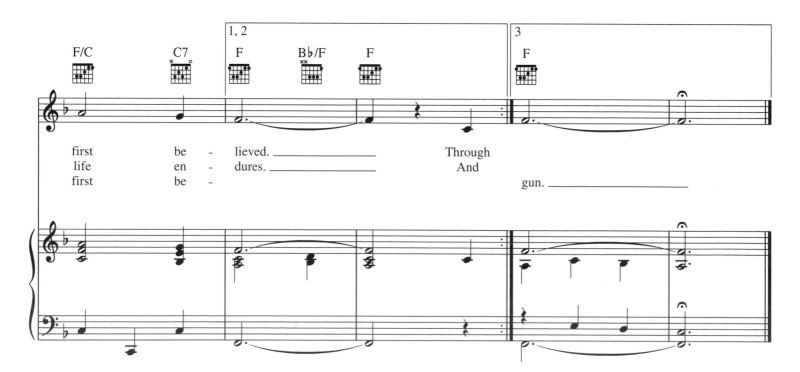

BECAUSE HE LIVES

Words by WILLIAM J. and GLORIA GAITHER
Music by WILLIAM J. GAITHER

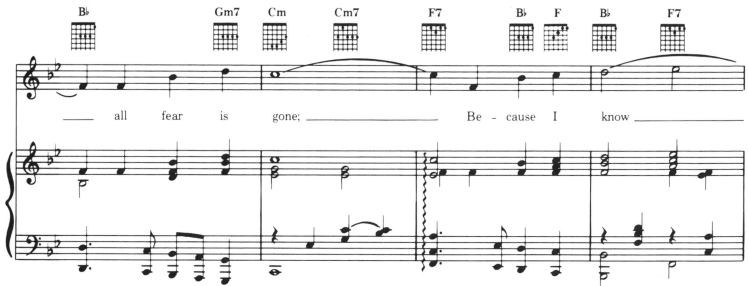

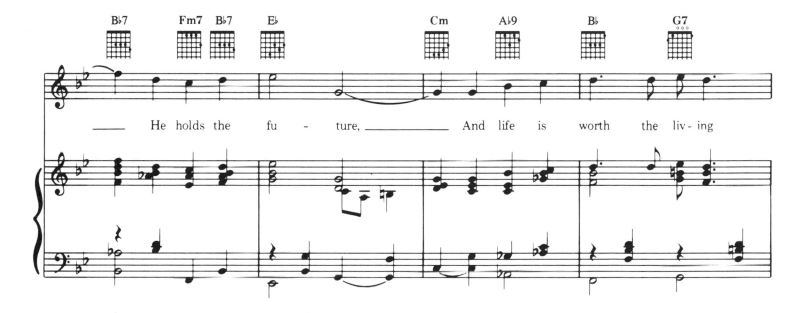

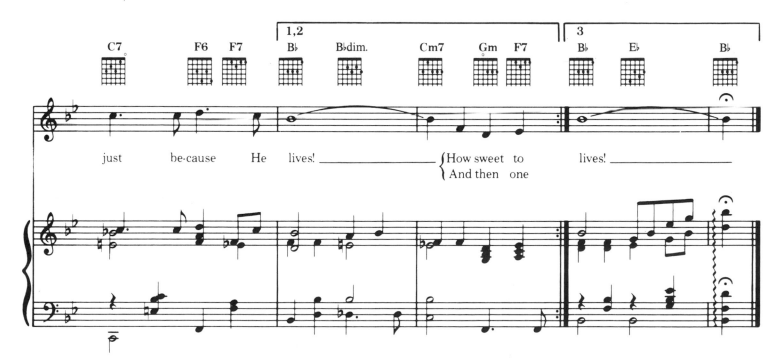

3. And then one day I'll cross that river;
I'll fight life's final war with pain;
And then as death gives way to vict'ry,
I'll see the lights of glory and I'll know He reigns.

AVE MARIA

By FRANZ SCHUBERT

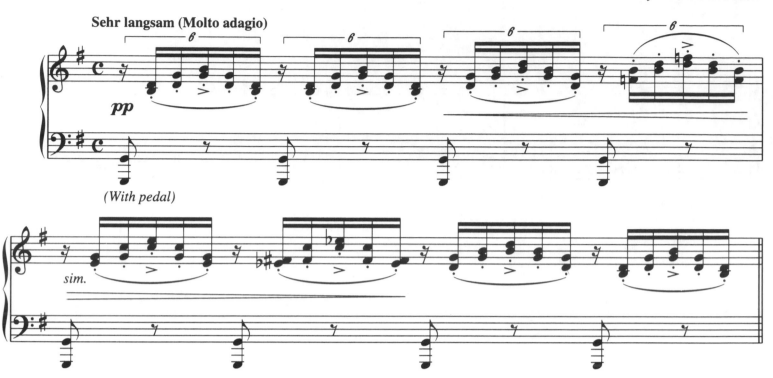

14

A - ve Ma - ri -
A - ve Ma - ri -

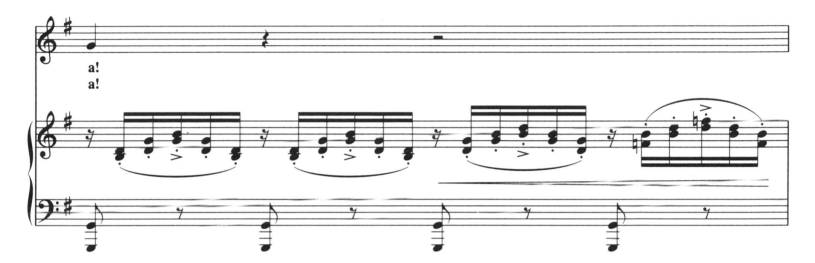

a!
a!

dim.

BEAUTIFUL ISLE OF SOMEWHERE

Words by JESSIE B. POUNDS
Music by JOHN S. FEARIS

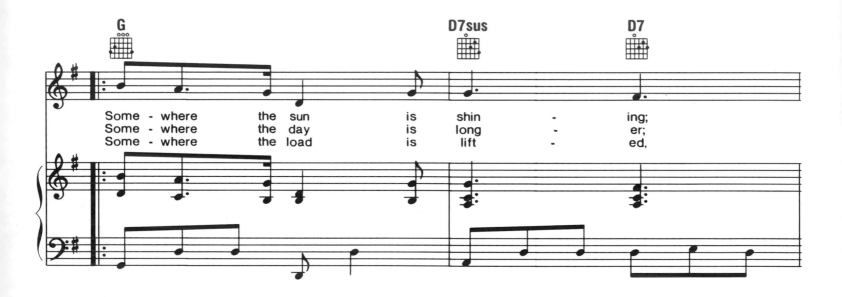

Some - where the sun is shin - ing;
Some - where the day is long - er;
Some - where the load is lift - ed,

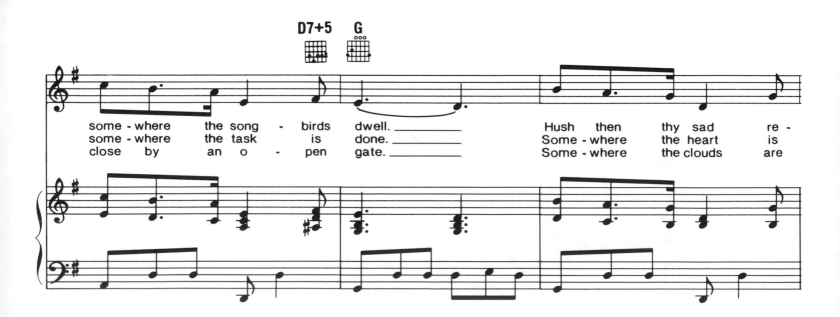

some - where the song - birds dwell. _____ Hush then thy sad re -
some - where the task is done. _____ Some - where the heart is
close by an o - pen gate. _____ Some - where the clouds are

BLESSED ASSURANCE

Lyrics by FANNY J. CROSBY
Music by PHOEBE PALMER KNAPP

With movement

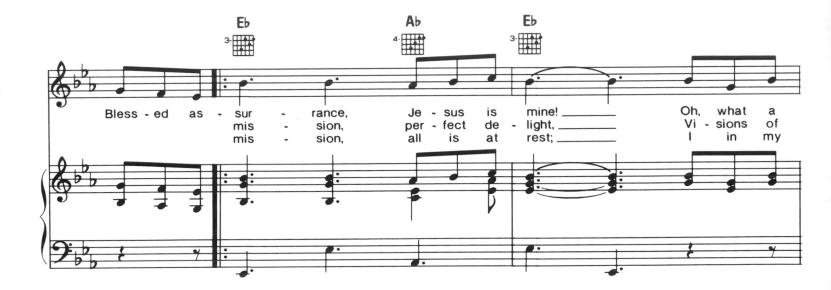

Bless - ed as - sur - rance, Je - sus is mine! _____ Oh, what a
mis - sion, per - fect de - light, _____ Vi - sions of
mis - sion, all is at rest; _____ I in my

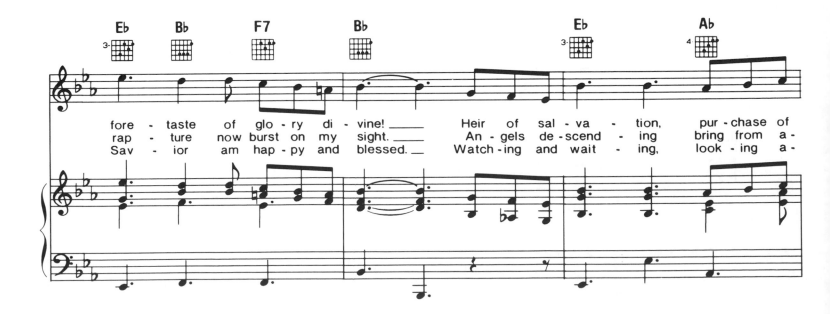

fore - taste of glo - ry di - vine! _____ Heir of sal - va - tion, pur - chase of
rap - ture now burst on my sight. _____ An - gels de - scend - ing bring from a -
Sav - ior am hap - py and blessed. _____ Watch - ing and wait - ing, look - ing a -

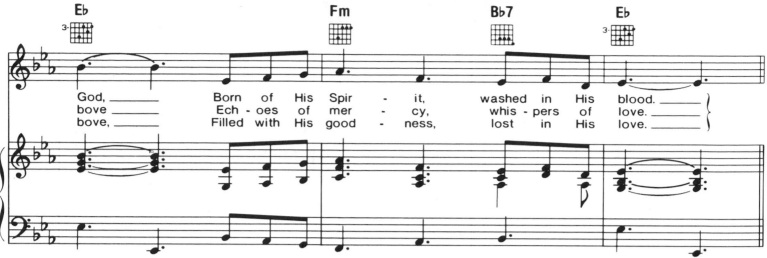

God, _____ Born of His Spir - it, washed in His blood. _____
bove _____ Ech - oes of mer - cy, whis - pers of love. _____
bove, _____ Filled with His good - ness, lost in His love. _____

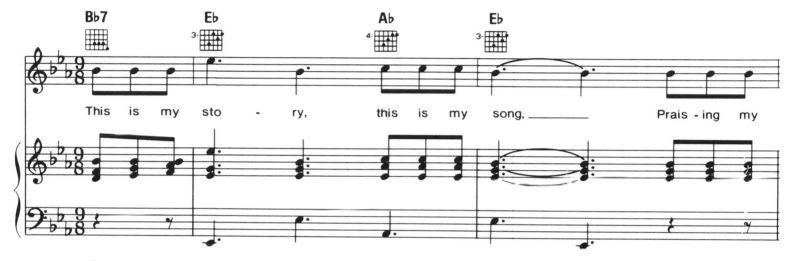

This is my sto - ry, this is my song, _____ Prais - ing my

Sav - ior all the day long. _____ This is my sto - ry this is my

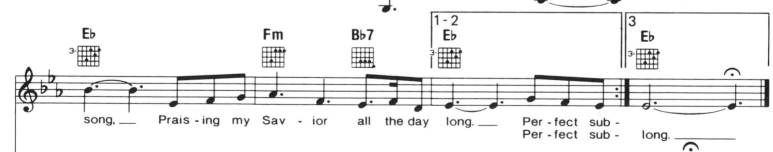

song, ___ Prais - ing my Sav - ior all the day long. ___ Per - fect sub -
Per - fect sub - long. _____

DEEP RIVER

African-American Spiritual
Based on Joshua 3

With emotion

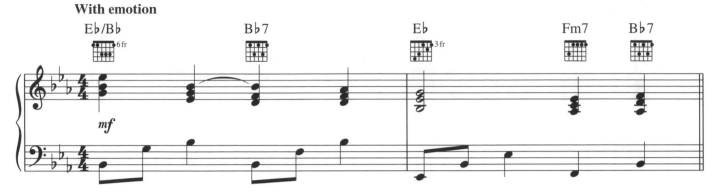

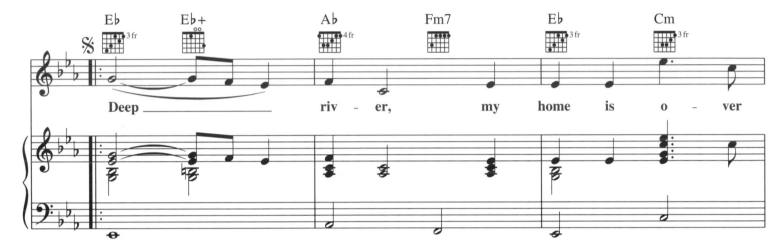

Deep _____ riv - er, my home is o - ver

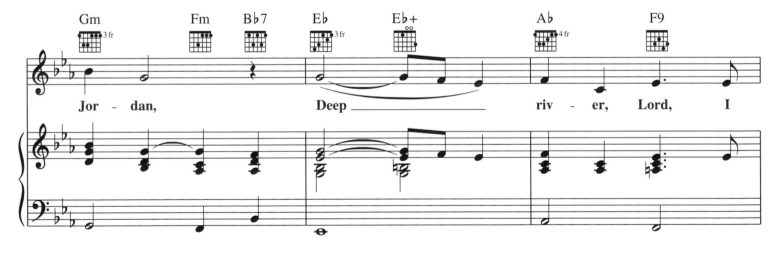

Jor - dan, Deep _____ riv - er, Lord, I

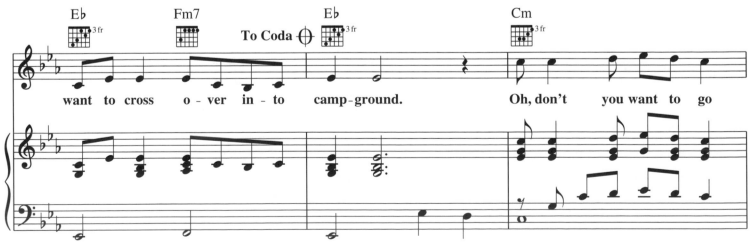

want to cross o - ver in - to camp-ground. Oh, don't you want to go

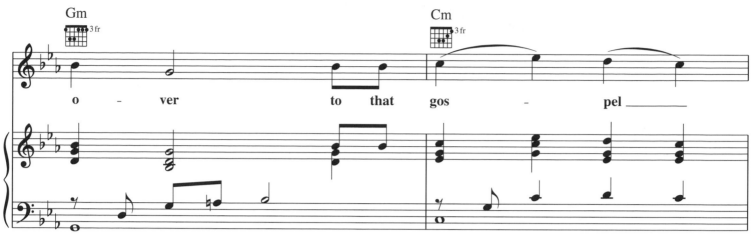

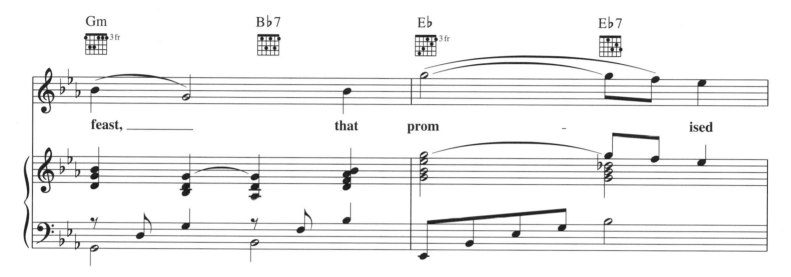

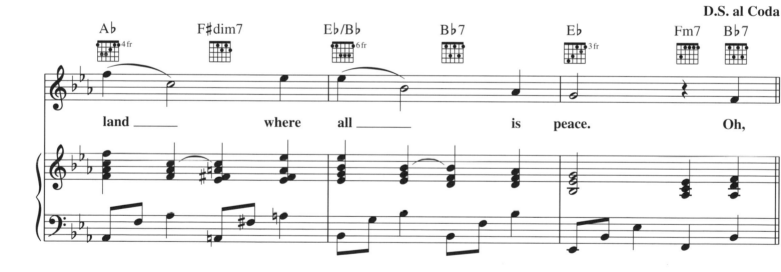

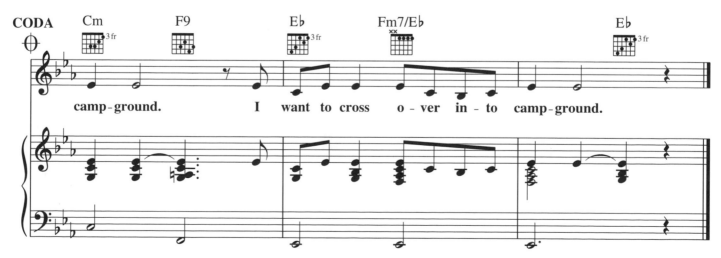

DOES JESUS CARE?

Words by FRANK E. GRAEFF
Music by J. LINCOLN HALL

long? _____
near? _____
long? _____
see? _____

O yes, He cares, I know He cares; His

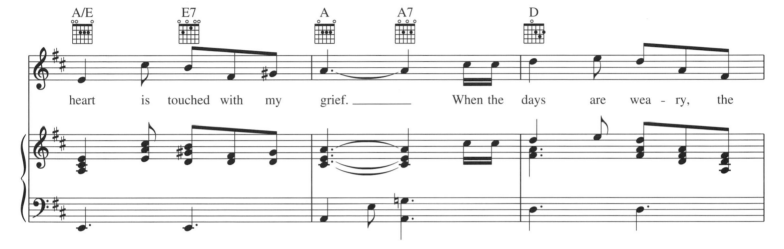

heart is touched with my grief. _____ When the days are wea-ry, the

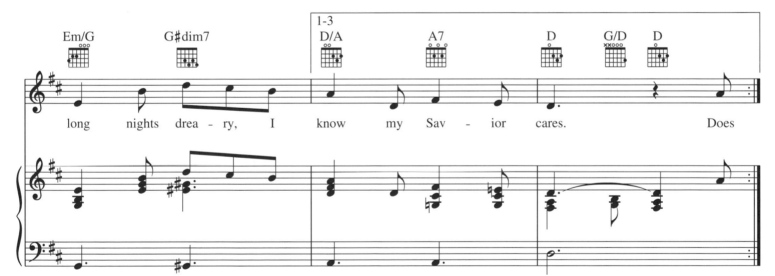

long nights drea-ry, I know my Sav-ior cares. Does

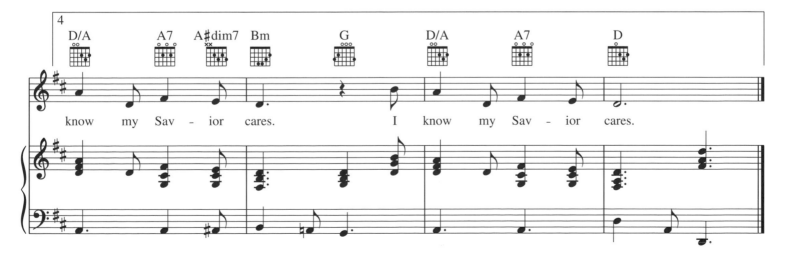

know my Sav-ior cares. I know my Sav-ior cares.

FOR ALL THE SAINTS

Words by WILLIAM W. HOW
Music by RALPH VAUGHAN WILLIAMS

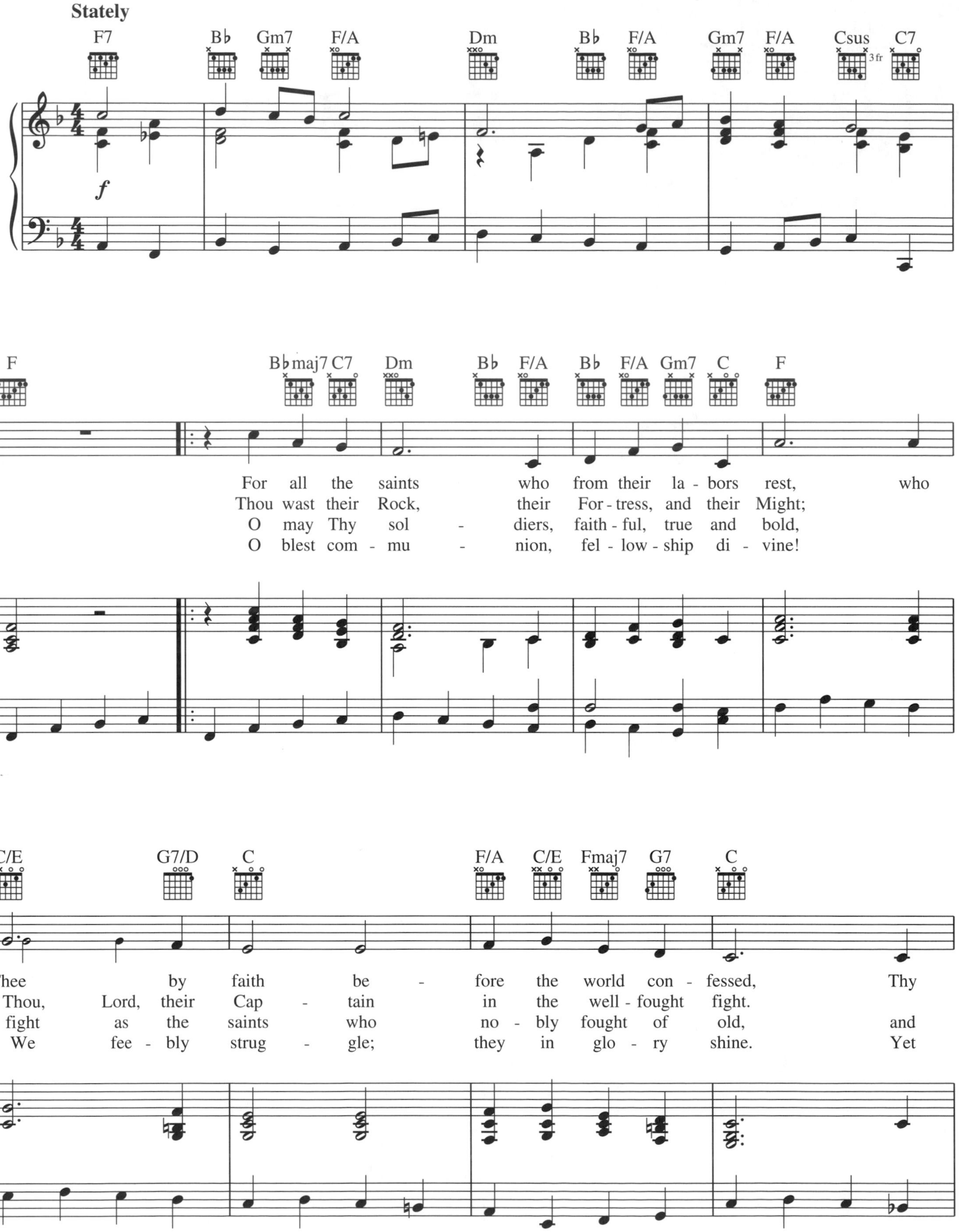

Stately
F7 B♭ Gm7 F/A Dm B♭ F/A Gm7 F/A Csus C7
3 fr
f
F B♭maj7 C7 Dm B♭ F/A B♭ F/A Gm7 C F
For all the saints who from their la - bors rest, who
Thou wast their Rock, their For - tress, and their Might;
O may Thy sol - diers, faith - ful, true and bold,
O blest com - mu - nion, fel - low - ship di - vine!
C/E G7/D C F/A C/E Fmaj7 G7 C
Thee by faith be - fore the world con - fessed, Thy
Thou, Lord, their Cap - tain in the well - fought fight.
fight as the saints who no - bly fought of old, and
We fee - bly strug - gle; they in glo - ry shine. Yet

name,   O   Je   -   sus,   be   for   -   ev   -   er
Thou,   in   the   dark   -   ness   drear,   their   one   true
win   with   them   one   the   vic   -   tor's   crown   of

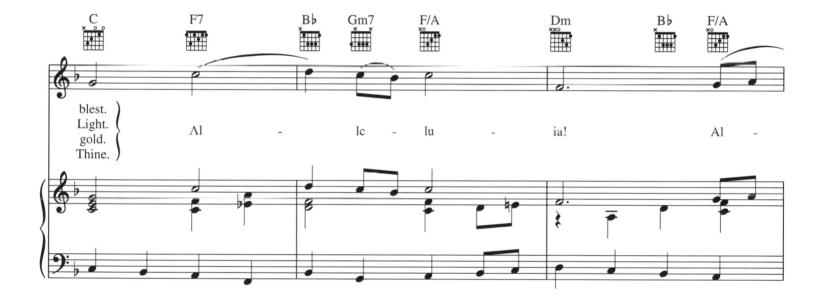

blest.   Light.   gold.   Thine.   Al   -   le   -   lu   -   ia!   Al   -

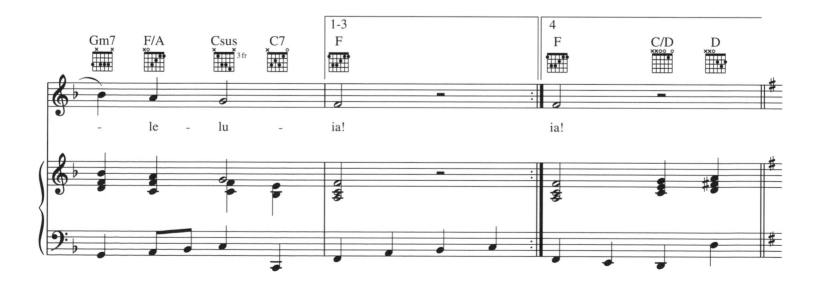

-   le   -   lu   -   ia!   ia!

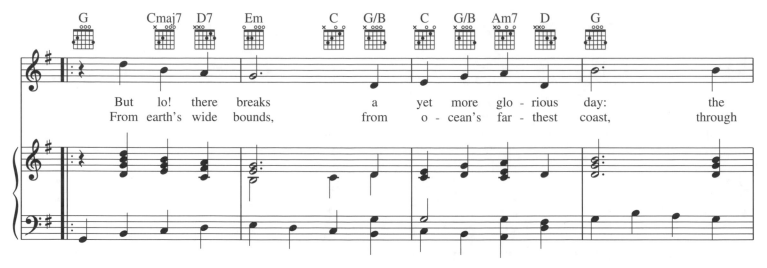

But lo! there breaks a yet more glo-rious day: the
From earth's wide bounds, from o-cean's far-thest coast, through

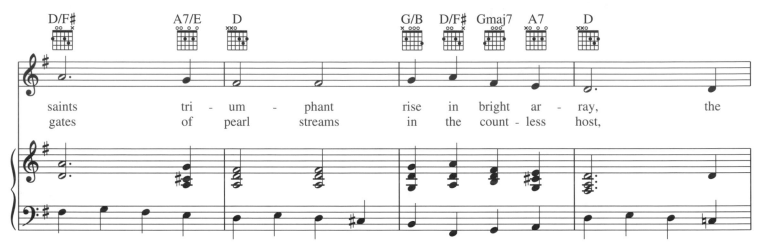

saints tri - um - phant rise in bright ar - ray, the
gates of pearl streams in the count - less host,

King of Glo - ry pass - es on ___ His ___ way. } Al -
sing - ing to Fa - ther, Son and Ho - ly ___ Ghost. }

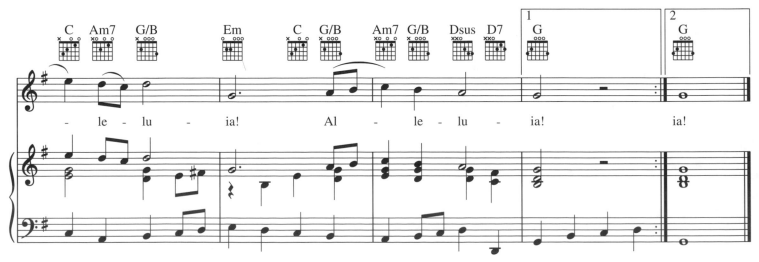

- le - lu - ia! Al - le - lu - ia! ia!

FRIENDS

Recorded by Michael W. Smith

Words and Music by MICHAEL W. SMITH
and DEBORAH D. SMITH

GIVE ME JESUS

African-American Spiritual

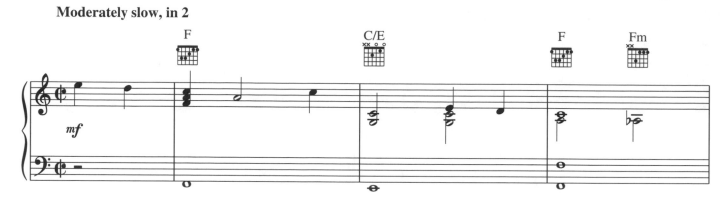

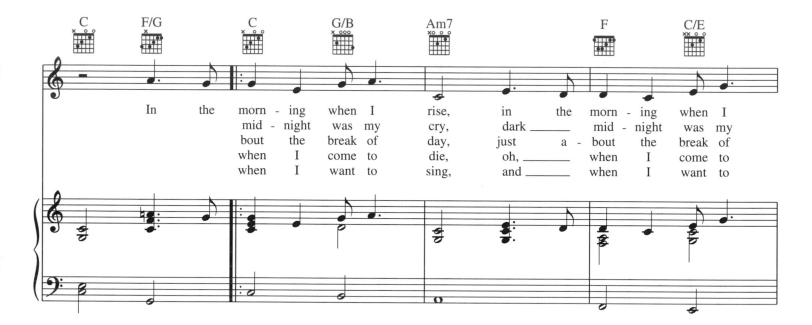

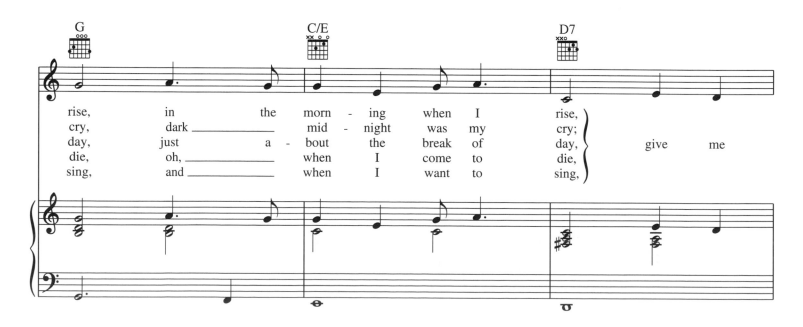

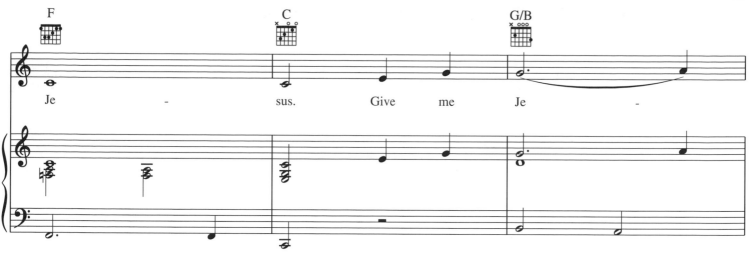

Je - sus. Give me Je -

sus, give me Je - sus. You may have all the

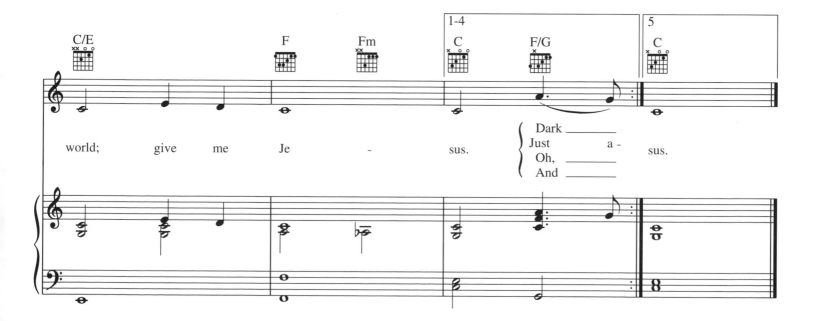

world; give me Je - sus.

Dark _____
Just a -
Oh, _____ sus.
And _____

HE SHALL FEED HIS FLOCK

Text adapted from the Book of Isaiah, 40:11
Music by GEORGE FRIDERIC HANDEL

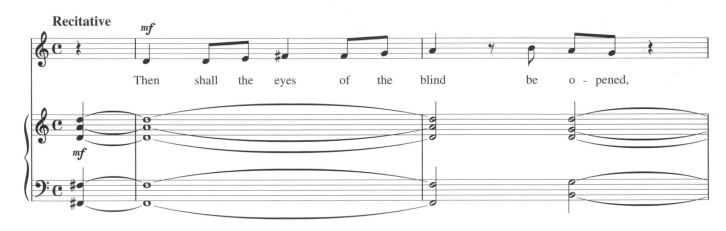

Then shall the eyes of the blind be o - pened,

and the ears of the deaf un - stop - ped, then shall the lame man leap as a

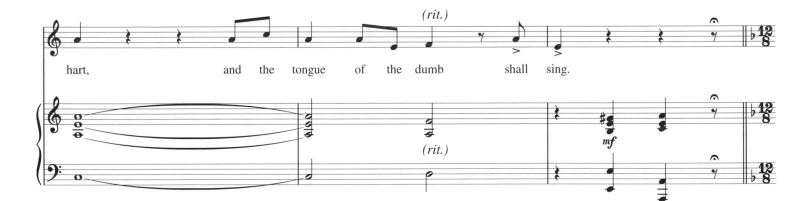

hart, and the tongue of the dumb shall sing.

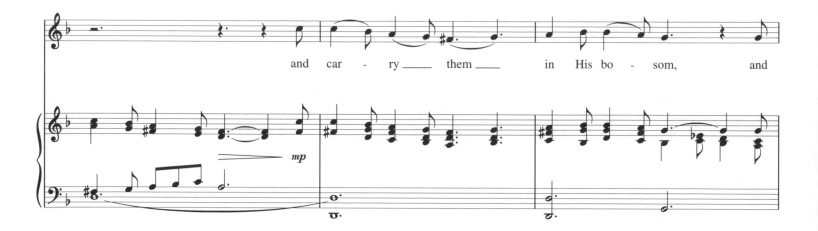

and car - ry _____ them _____ in His bo - som, and

gent - ly lead _____ those _____ that are _____ with young, _____ and

gent - ly lead _____ those, _____ and gent - ly lead _____ those that

are _____ with young.

HOW GREAT THOU ART

Words and Music by
STUART K. HINE

*Author's original words are "works" and "mighty."

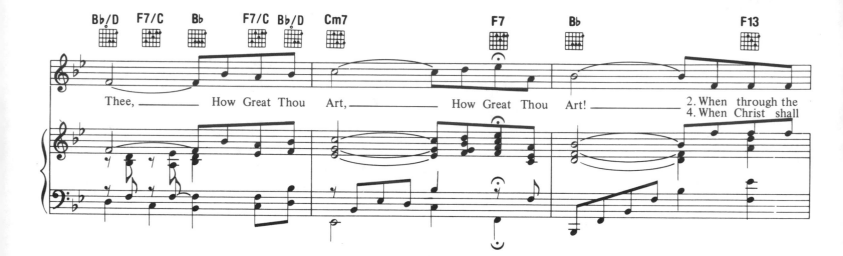

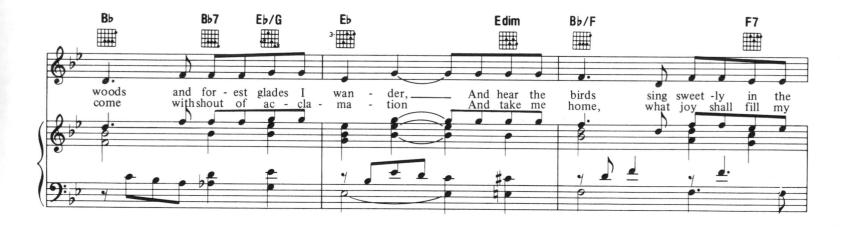

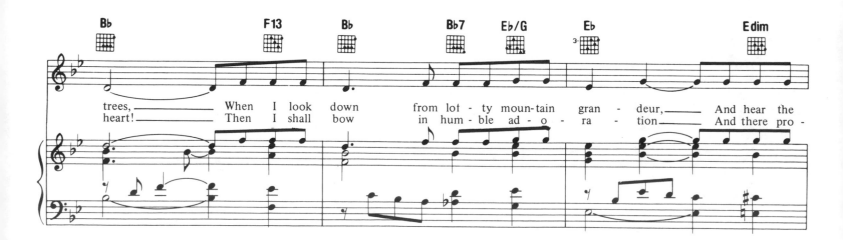

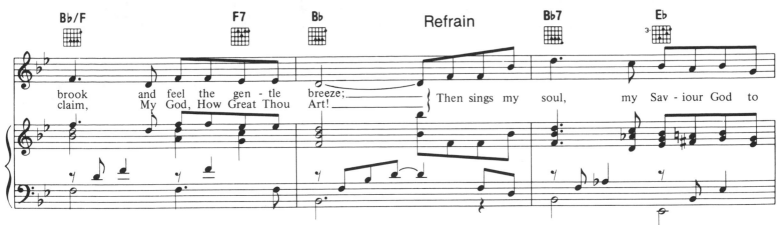

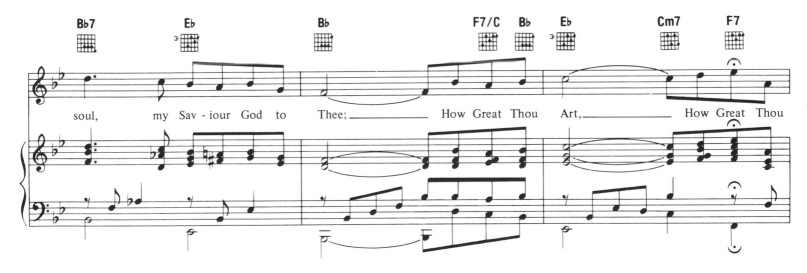
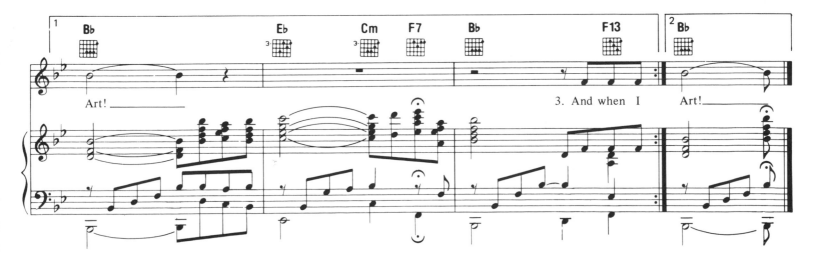

HE THE PEARLY GATES WILL OPEN

Words by FREDRICK A. BLOM
Translated by NATHANIEL CARLSON
Music by ELSIE AHLWEN

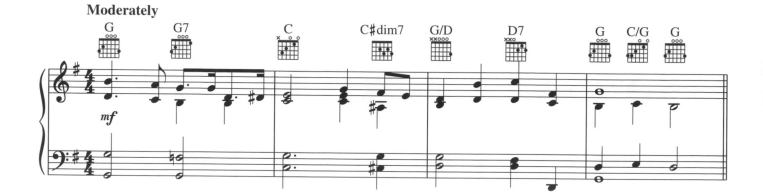

Love   di-vine, so great and won - drous,   deep   and might-y, pure, sub-lime,
Like   a dove when hunt-ed, fright - ened,   as   a wound-ed fawn was I.
Love   di-vine, so great and won - drous!   All   my sins He then for-gave.
In   life's e-ven-tide, at twi - light,   at   His door I'll knock and wait.

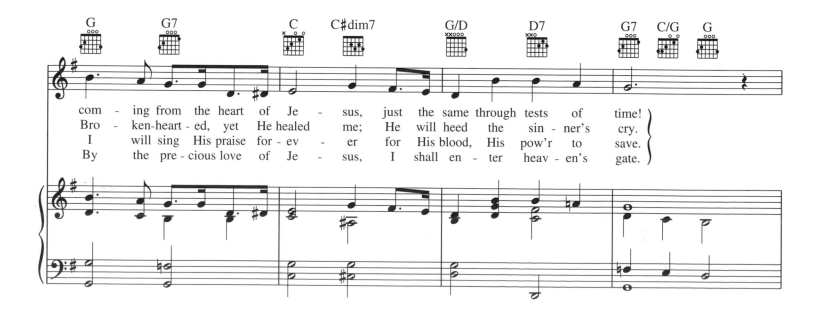

com - ing from the heart of Je - sus,   just   the same through tests   of   time!
Bro - ken-heart-ed, yet He healed   me;   He   will heed the sin-ner's   cry.
I   will sing His praise for-ev - er   for   His blood, His pow'r to   save.
By   the pre-cious love of Je - sus,   I   shall en-ter heav-en's   gate.

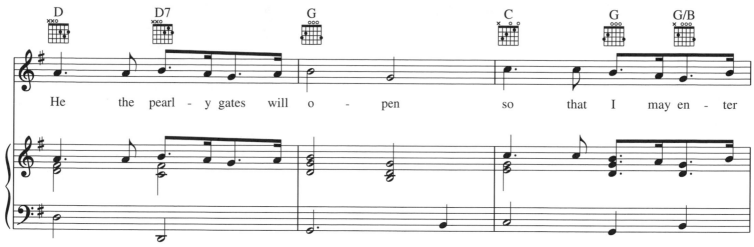

He the pearl - y gates will o - pen so that I may en - ter

in, for He pur - chased my re - demp - tion and for -

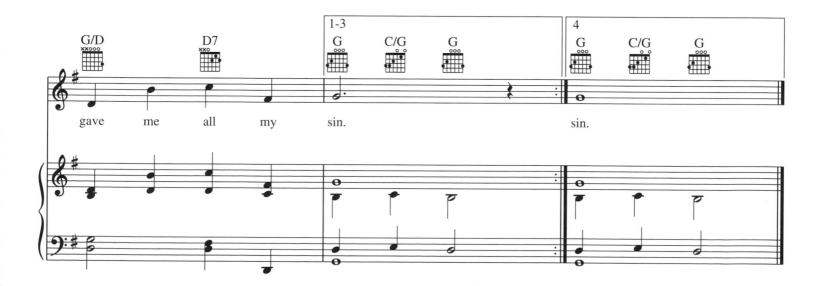

gave me all my sin. sin.

HIS EYE IS ON THE SPARROW

Words by CIVILLA D. MARTIN
Music by CHARLES H. GABRIEL

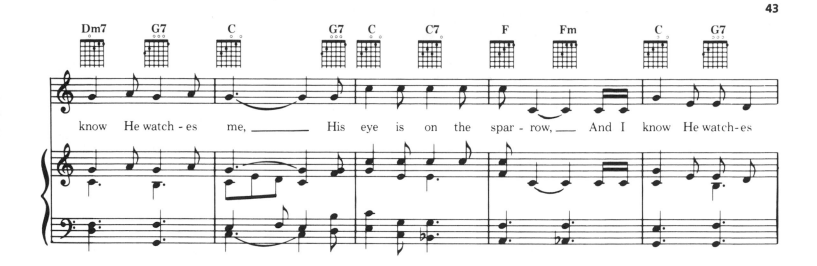

know He watch-es me, _____ His eye is on the spar-row, ____ And I know He watch-es

Chorus

me. ___ I sing be-cause I'm hap-py, _____ I sing be-cause I'm free; _____ For His

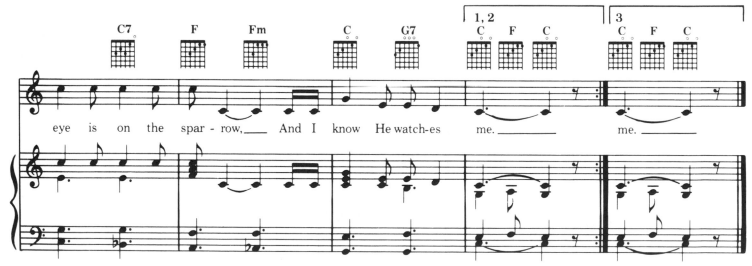

1, 2 **3**

eye is on the spar-row, ____ And I know He watch-es me. _____ me. _____

3. Whenever I am tempted,
Whenever clouds arise.
When song gives place to sighing,
When hope within me dies.
I draw the closer to Him,
From care He sets me free:

HOME FREE
Recorded by Wayne Watson

Words and Music by
WAYNE WATSON

Easy ♩ = 80

1. I'm try-ing

hard not to think You un-kind,———— but Heav-en-ly Fa-

-ther,———— if You know my heart, sure-ly You can read my mind.

Good peo-ple un-der-neath a sea of grief. Some

get up and walk—— a-way,—— some will find ul-ti-mate—— re-lief.————

Home free,___ e - ven - tu - al - ly;___ at the

ul - ti - mate__ heal - ing we will be home__ free.__ Home free,__ oh,

I've got a feel - ing,__ at the ul - ti - mate__ heal - ing we will be home__

free.__

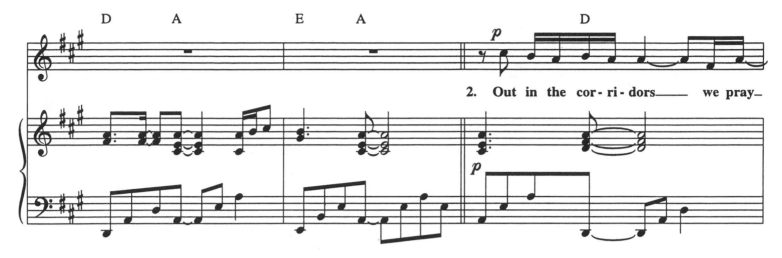

2. Out in the cor-ri-dors____ we pray____

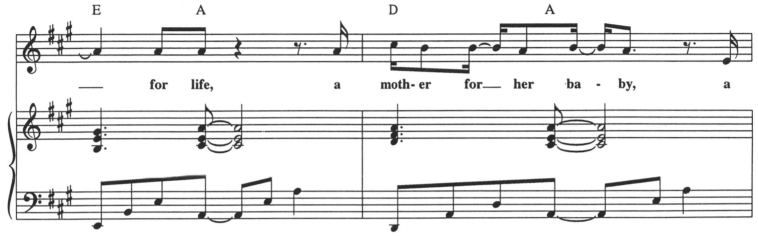

____ for life, a moth-er for____ her ba-by, a

hus-band for his wife.____ Oh,____ some-times the good____ die____ young; it's

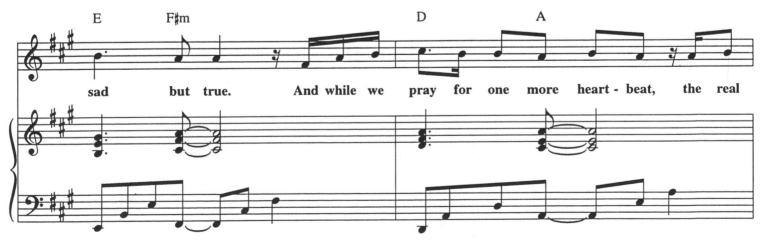

sad but true. And while we pray for one more heart-beat, the real

com - fort is___ with___ You._____ You know,

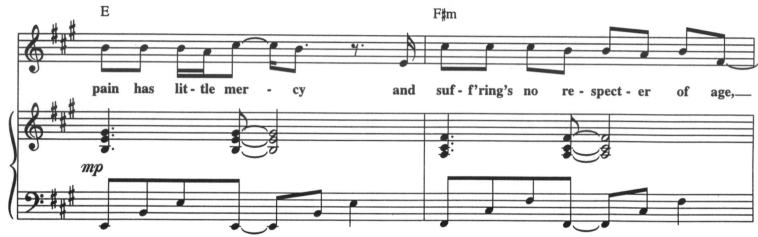

pain has lit - tle mer - cy and suf - f'ring's no re - spect - er of age,___

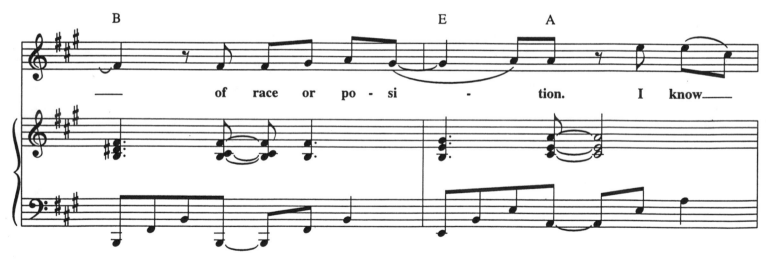

___ of race or po - si - tion. I know___

ev - 'ry prayer___ gets an - swered but the hard - est one to pray___ is slow to come.___

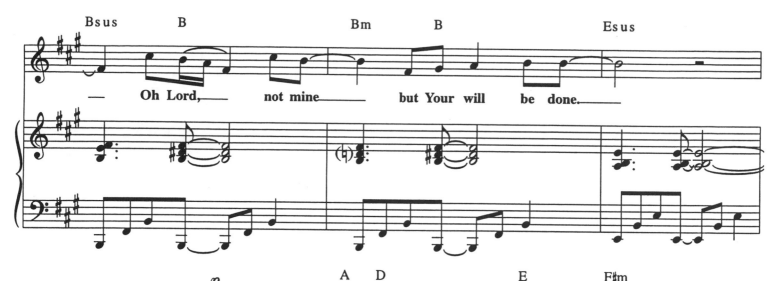

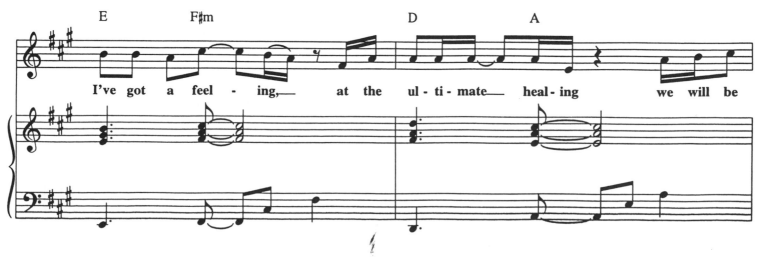

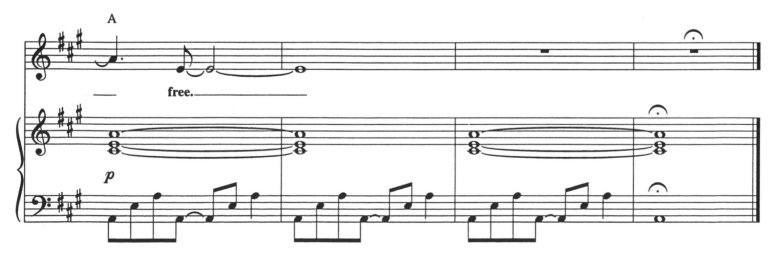

I WALKED TODAY WHERE JESUS WALKED

By GEOFFREY O'HARA
and DANIEL TWOHIG

walked to-day where Je-sus walked, __ In days of long a - go; I wan -dered down each path He knew, __ With rev-'rent step and slow. Those

* Words used by exclusive permission

lit - tle lanes, they have not changed— A sweet peace fills the

air. I walked to-day where Je- sus walked, _____ And

felt His pres - ence there. My

Allegretto

path-way led through Beth - le - hem, _____ Ah! mem-'ries

ev - - er sweet; The

lit - tle hills of Gal - i - lee, _____ That knew those

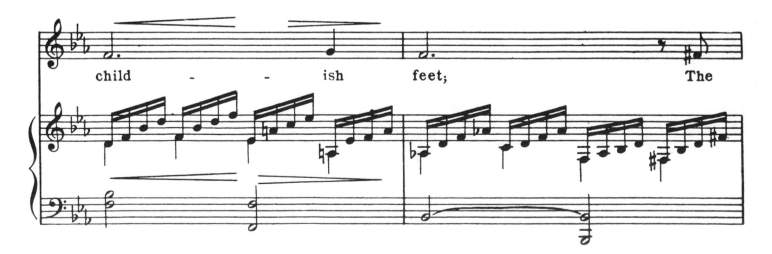

child - - ish feet; The

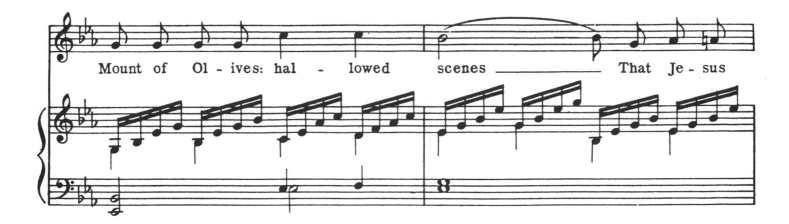

Mount of Ol - ives: hal - lowed scenes _____ That Je - sus

knew be - fore; I

saw the might - y Jor - dan roll _____ As in the

days of yore.

I knelt to-day where Je-sus knelt, ___ Where

all a-lone He prayed; The Gar - den of Geth-sem - a -

ne-___ My heart felt un - a - fraid! I

picked my heav-y bur-den up ___ And with Him by my

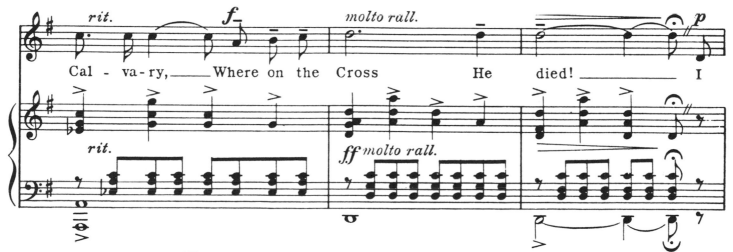

I'LL FLY AWAY

Words and Music by
ALBERT E. BRUMLEY

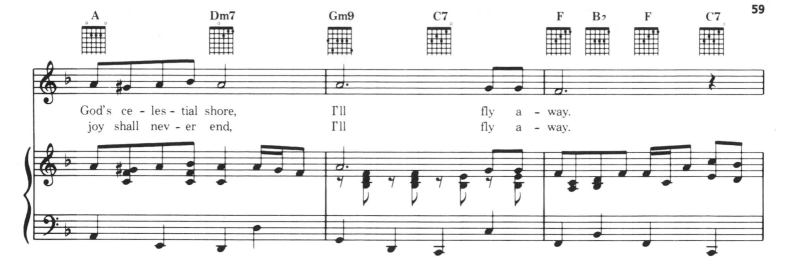

God's ce-les-tial shore,   I'll   fly a-way.
joy shall nev-er end,   I'll   fly a-way.

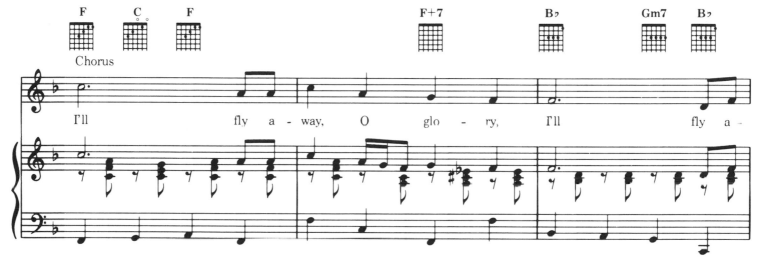

Chorus

I'll   fly a-way, O glo-ry, I'll   fly a-

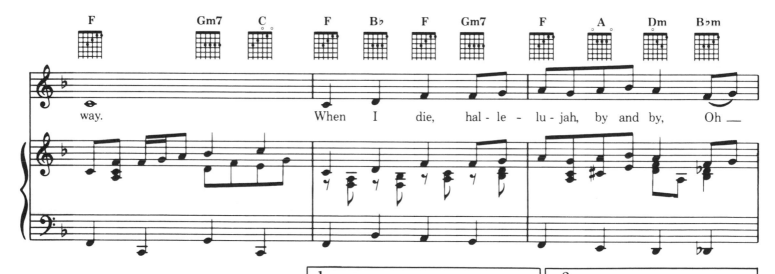

way.   When I die, hal-le-lu-jah, by and by,   Oh —

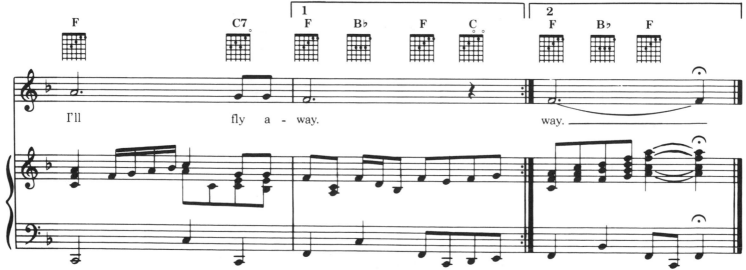

I'll   fly a-way.   way. —

IF YOU COULD SEE ME NOW

Recorded by Truth

Words and Music by
KIM NOBLITT

Very slowly and freely

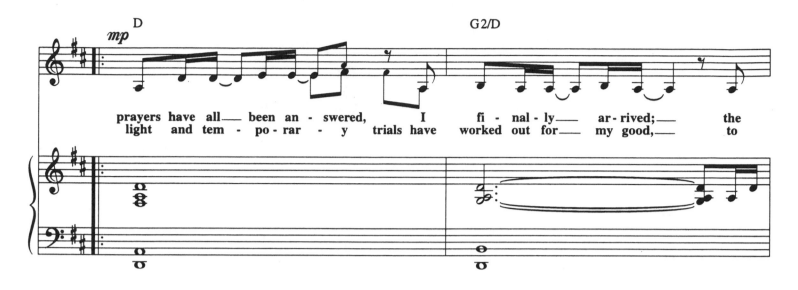

prayers have all— been an - swered, I fi - nal - ly— ar - rived;— the
light and tem - po - rar - y trials have worked out for— my good,— to

heal - ing that— had been— de - layed— has now been re - al - ized.—
know it brought— Him glo - ry— when I mis - un - der - stood.—

No one's in— a hur - ry, there's no sched - ule— to— keep;— we're
Though we've had— our sor - rows, they can nev - er— com - pare. What

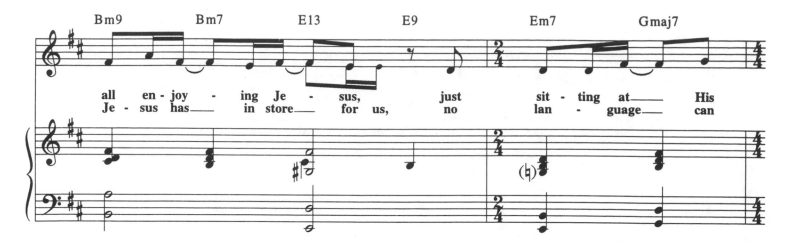

all en - joy - ing Je - sus, just sit - ting at___ His
Je - sus has___ in store___ for us, no lan - guage___ can

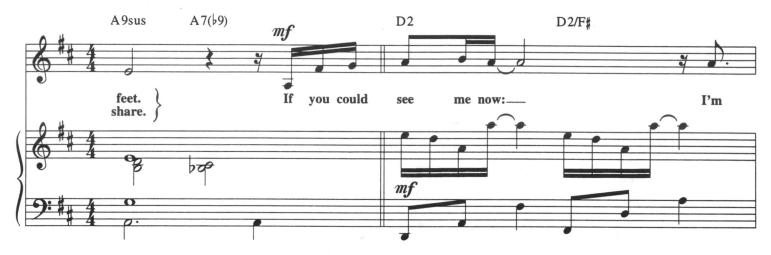

feet.
share.

If you could see me now:___ I'm

walk - ing streets___ of gold.___ If you could see me now:___ I'm

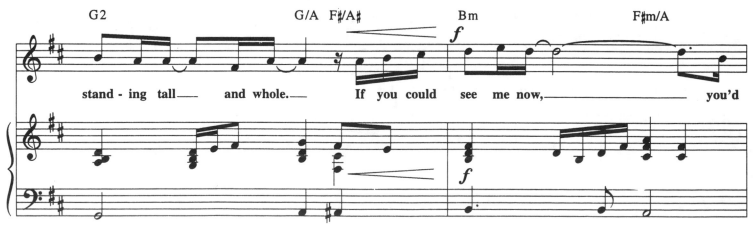

stand - ing tall___ and whole.___ If you could see me now,_____ you'd

know I've seen His face. If you could see me now, you'd

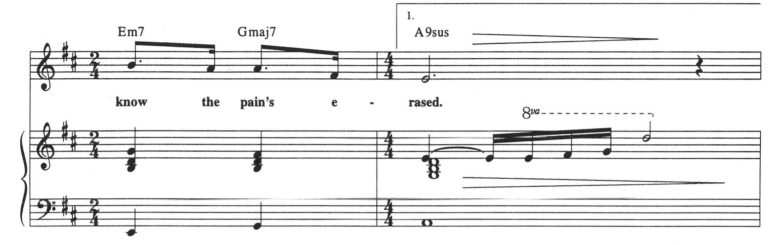

1.

know the pain's e - rased.

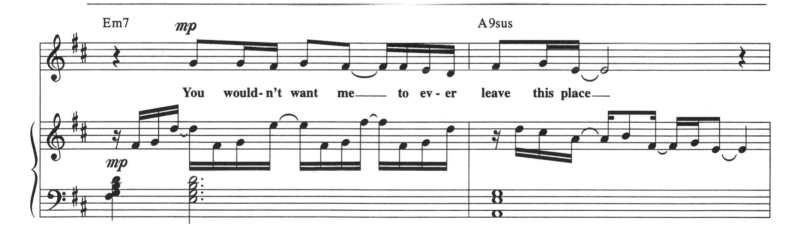

You would-n't want me to ev - er leave this place

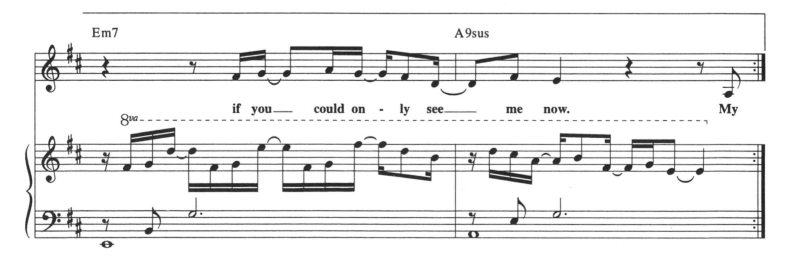

if you could on - ly see me now. My

me now,   if you could on - ly

see me now.

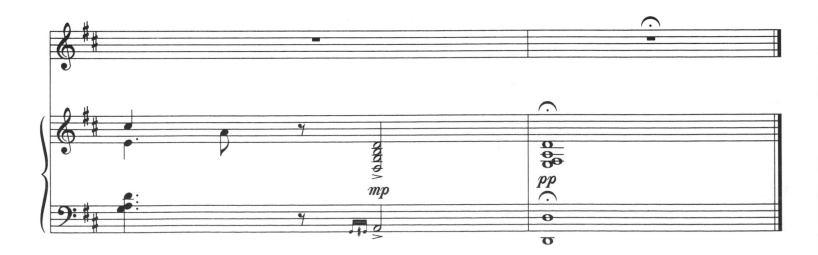

IVORY PALACES

Words and Music by
HENRY BARRACLOUGH

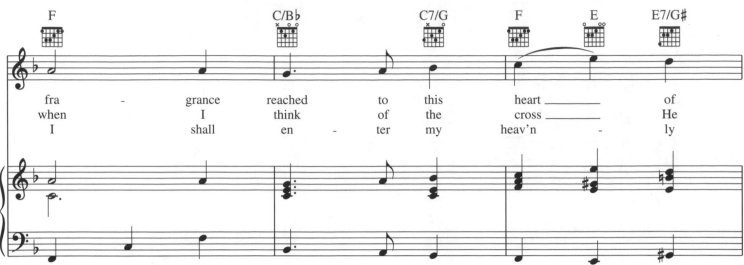

fra - grance reached to this heart _____ of
when I think of the cross _____ He
I shall en - ter my heav'n - ly

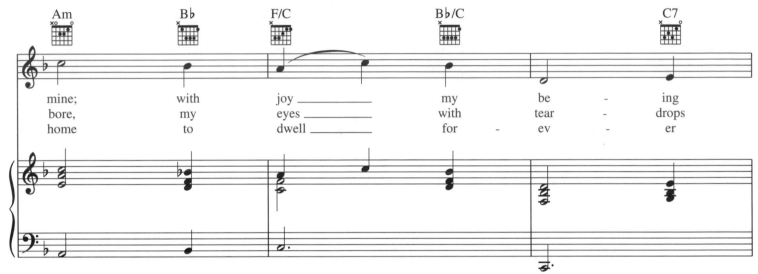

mine; with joy _____ my be - ing
bore, my eyes _____ with tear - drops
home to dwell _____ for - ev - er

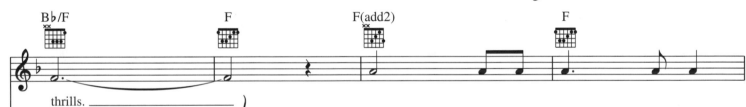

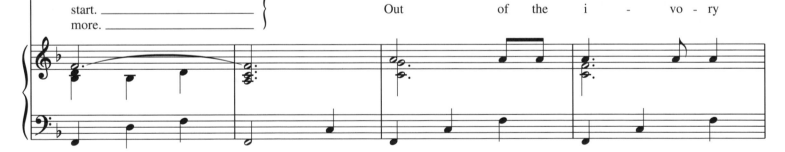

thrills. _____
start. _____ } Out of the i - vo - ry
more. _____

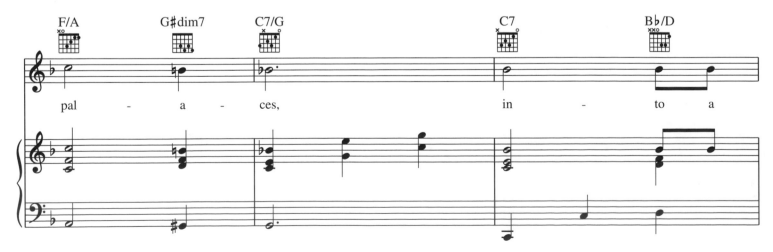

pal - a - ces, in - to a

world of woe; _____ on - ly His

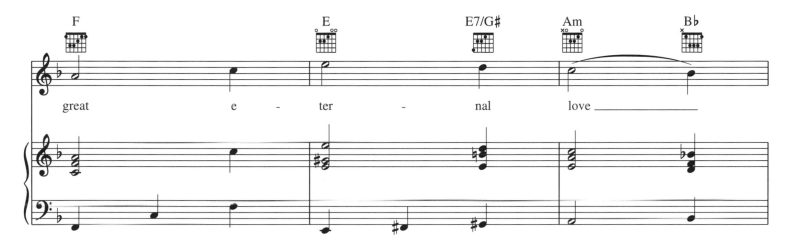

great e - ter - nal love _____

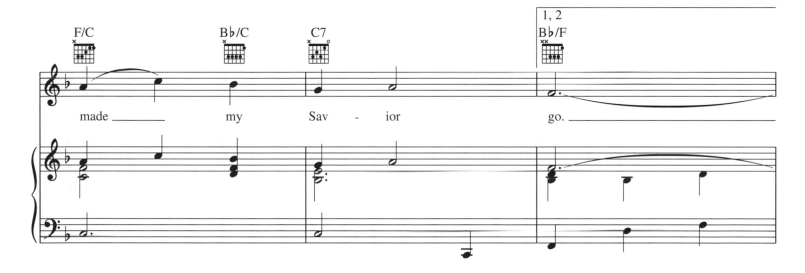

made _____ my Sav - ior go. _____

1, 2

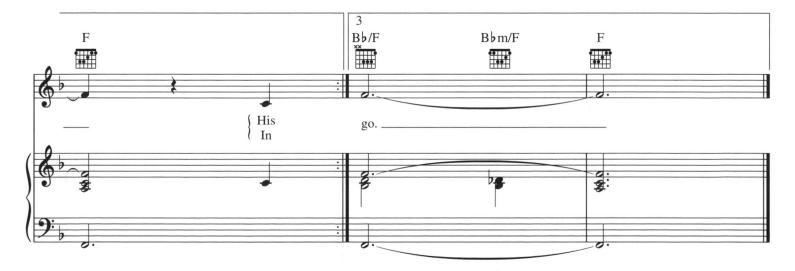

His
In

go. _____

IN THE GARDEN

Words and Music by
C. AUSTIN MILES

Flowing

I come to the gar - den a - lone, _____ while the
speaks, and the sound of His voice _____ is so

dew is still on the ros - es; and the voice I
sweet the birds hush their sing - ing; and the mel - o -

hear, fall - ing on my ear, the Son of God dis -
-dy that He gave to me with - in my heart is

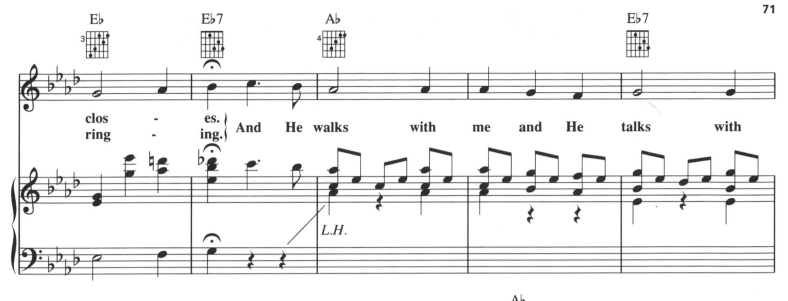

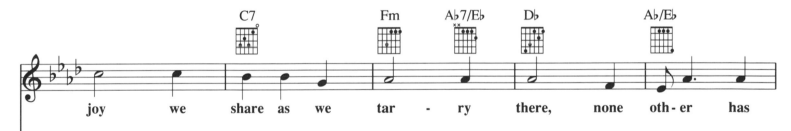

IT IS WELL WITH MY SOUL

Words by HORATIO G. SPAFFORD
Music by PHILIP P. BLISS

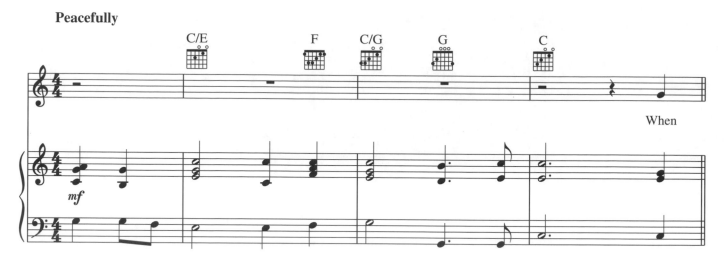

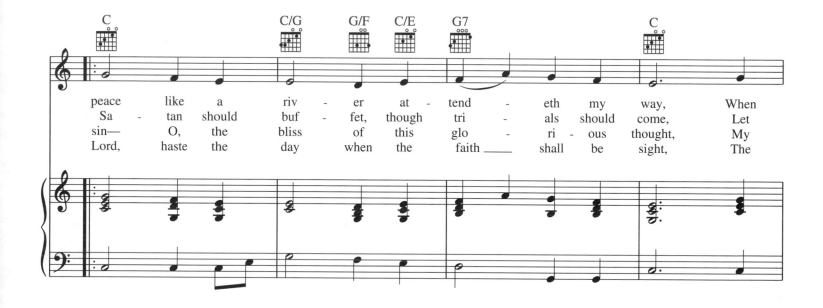

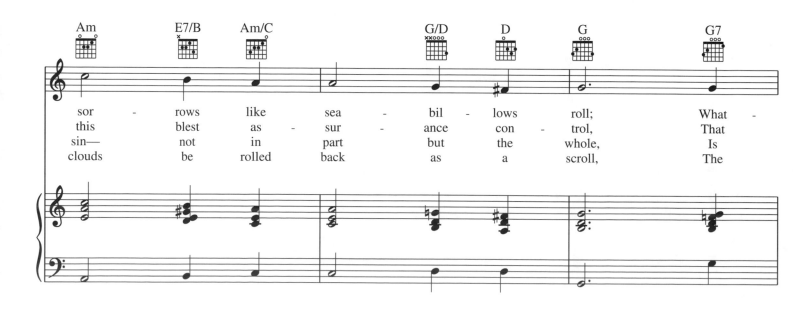

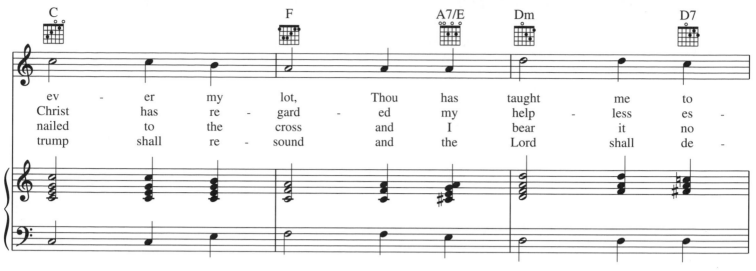

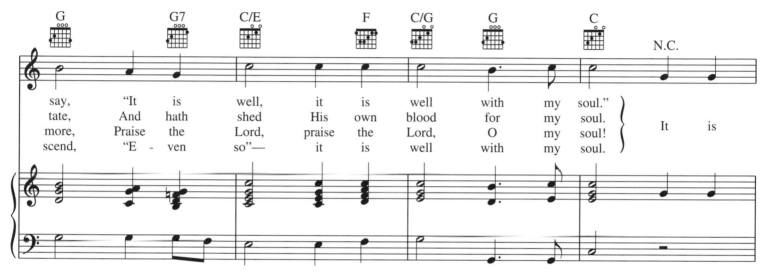

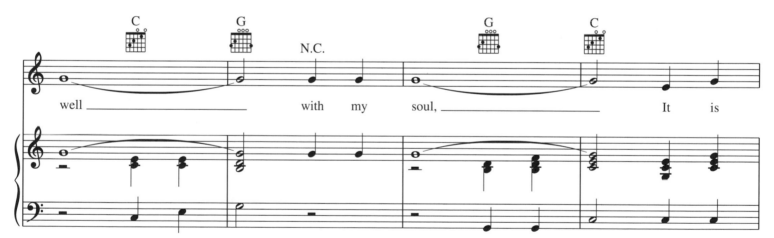

JESUS WILL STILL BE THERE
Recorded by Point of Grace

Words and Music by ROBERT STERLING
and JOHN MANDEVILLE

Things change, __ plans fail, __ you look for love __ on a grand-
Time flies, __ hearts turn __ a lit-tle bit wis- er from les-

- er scale. __ Storms rise, __ hopes fade, __ and
- sons learned. __ But some-times __ weak- ness __ wins, __ and

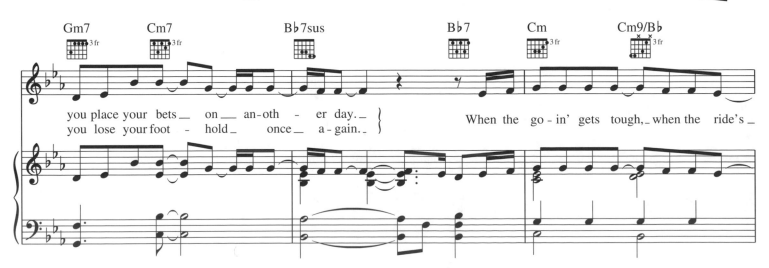

you place your bets __ on __ an-oth- er day. __
you lose your foot- hold __ once __ a-gain. __

When the go-in' gets tough, __ when the ride's __

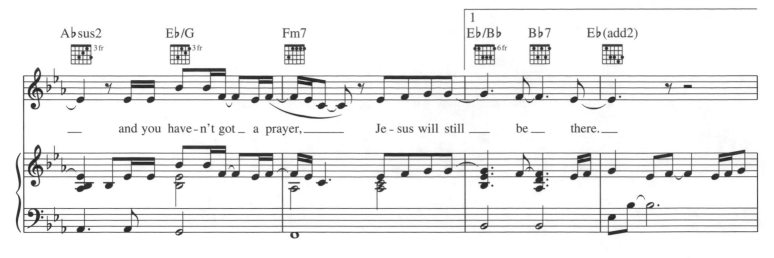

and you have-n't got __ a prayer, _____ Je - sus will still ___ be ___ there. __

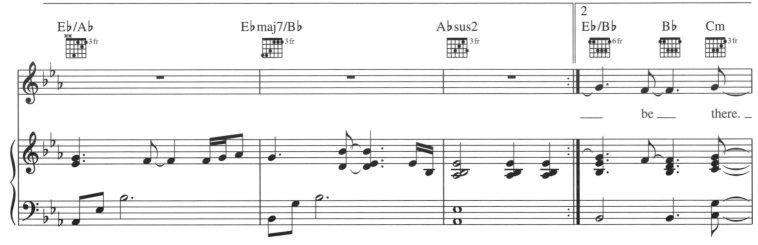

__ be ___ there. __

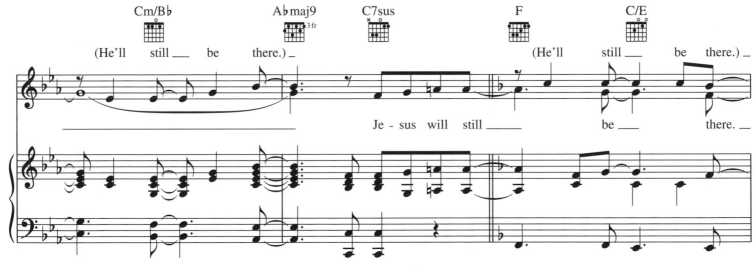

(He'll still ___ be there.) _ _____ (He'll still ___ be there.) _

Je - sus will still _____ be ___ there. __

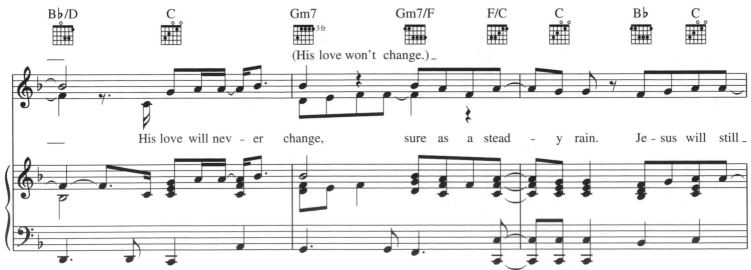

(His love won't change.) _

__ His love will nev - er change, sure as a stead - y rain. Je - sus will still _

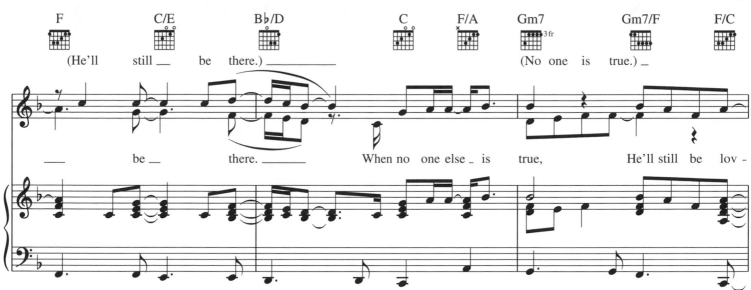

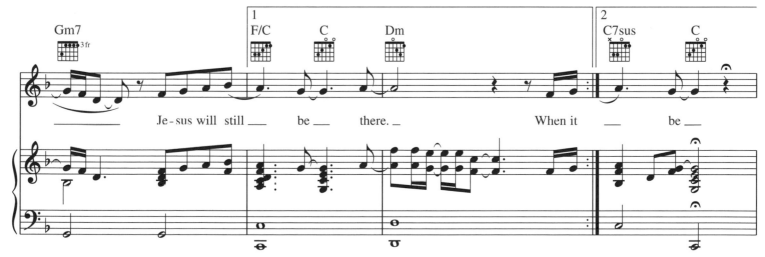

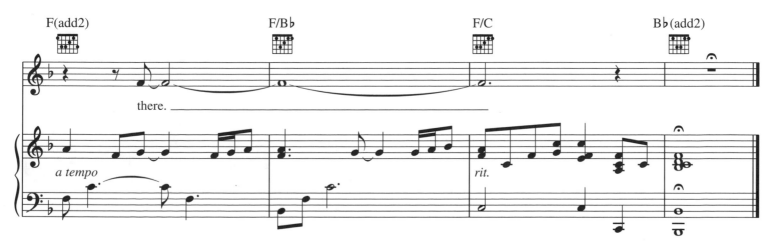

JUST A CLOSER WALK WITH THEE

Traditional
Arranged by KENNETH MORRIS

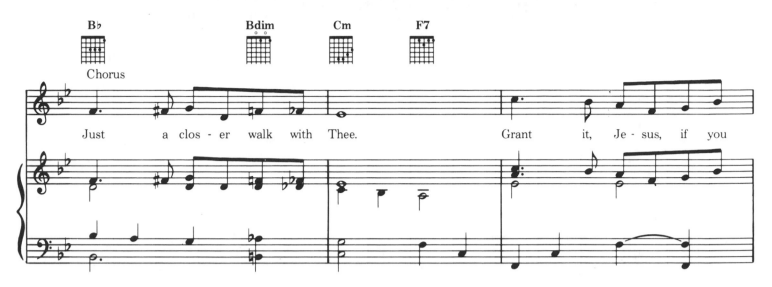

Chorus

Just a clos-er walk with Thee. Grant it, Je-sus, if you

please; _____ Dai - ly walk-ing close to Thee _____ Let it

be, dear Lord, let it be! be!

3. When my feeble life is o'er,
Time for me will be no more;
On that bright eternal shore
I will walk, dear Lord, close to Thee.

THE LORD'S PRAYER

By ALBERT H. MALOTTE

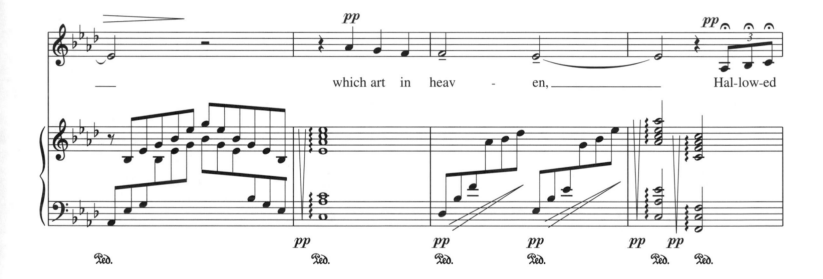

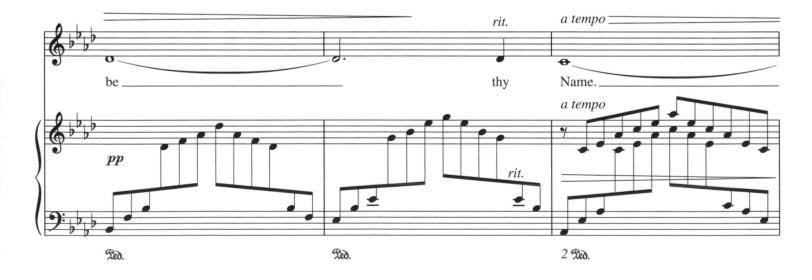

MY SAVIOR FIRST OF ALL

Words by FANNY J. CROSBY
Music by JOHN R. SWENEY

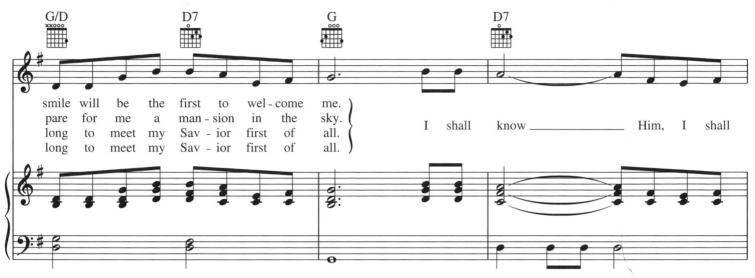

smile will be the first to wel-come me.
pare for me a man-sion in the sky.
long to meet my Sav-ior first of all.
long to meet my Sav-ior first of all.

I shall know _____ Him, I shall

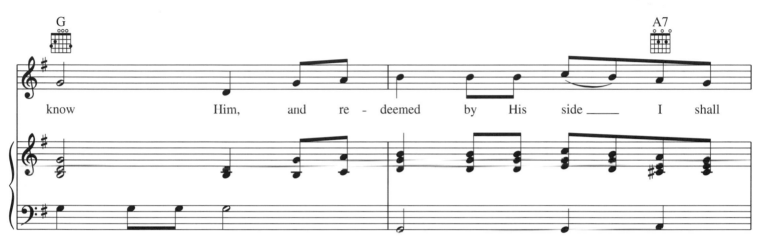

know Him, and re-deemed by His side ____ I shall

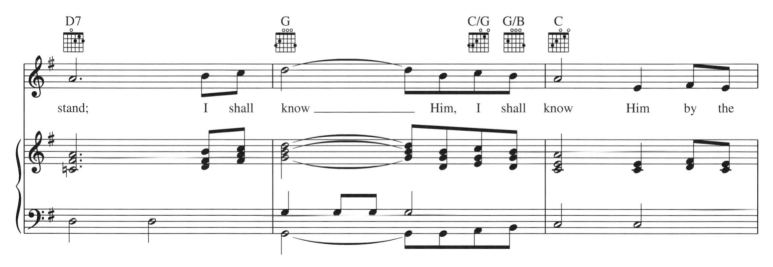

stand; I shall know _____ Him, I shall know Him by the

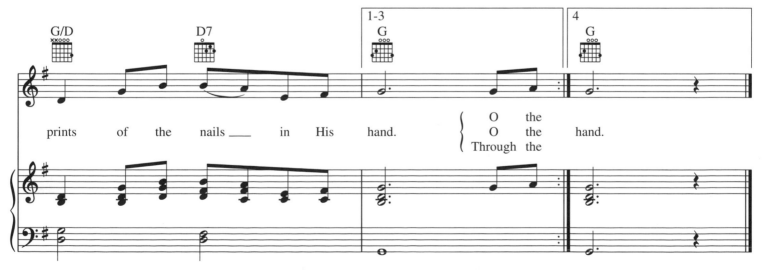

prints of the nails ___ in His hand.

1-3
O the
O the hand.
Through the

O THAT WILL BE GLORY

Words and Music by
CHARLES H. GABRIEL

Flowing, with joy

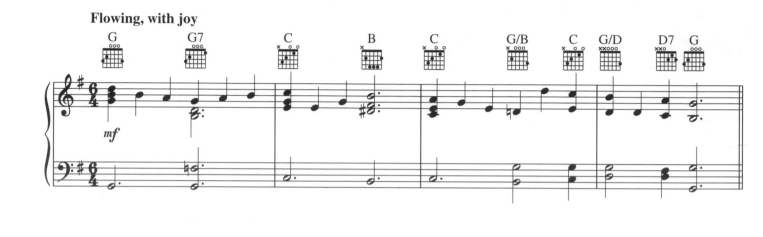

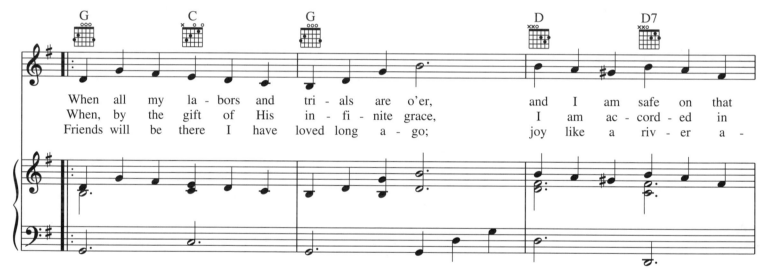

When all my la - bors and tri - als are o'er, and I am safe on that
When, by the gift of His in - fi - nite grace, I am ac - cord - ed in
Friends will be there I have loved long a - go; joy like a riv - er a -

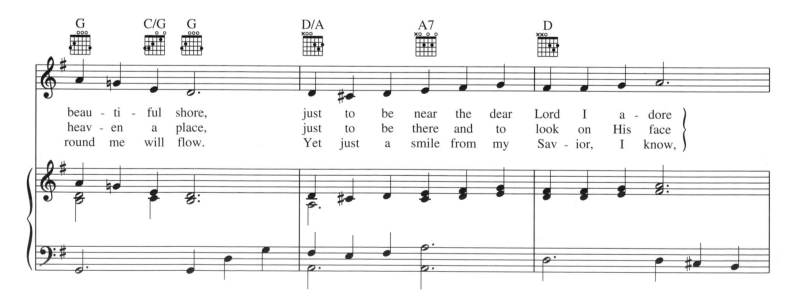

beau - ti - ful shore, just to be near the dear Lord I a - dore
heav - en a place, just to be there and to look on His face
round me will flow. Yet just a smile from my Sav - ior, I know,

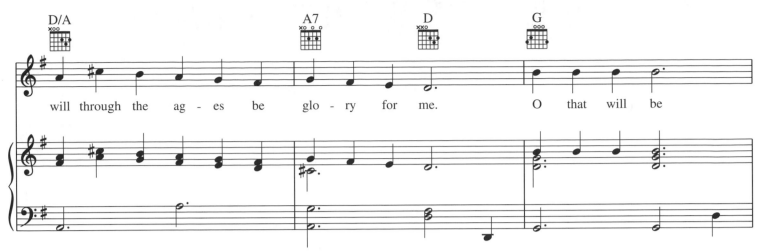

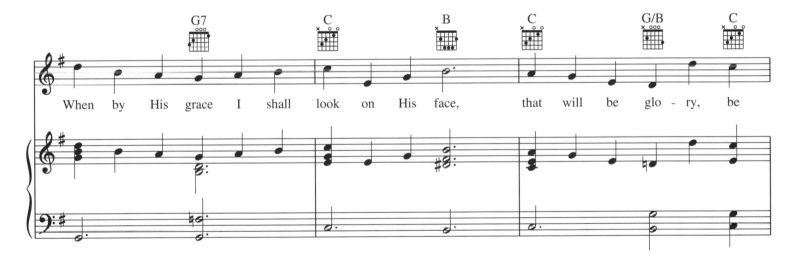

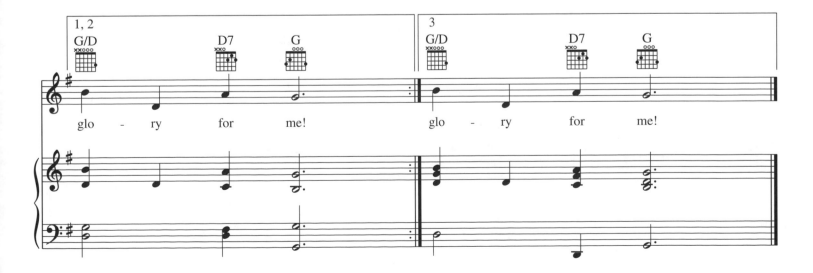

ON JORDAN'S STORMY BANKS

Words by SAMUEL STENNETT
Traditional American Melody

hap - py land where __ my pos - ses - sions lie.
ev - er reigns and __ scat - ters __ night a - way.
pain and death are __ felt and __ feared no more.
Fa - ther's face and __ in His __ bo - som rest?

I am

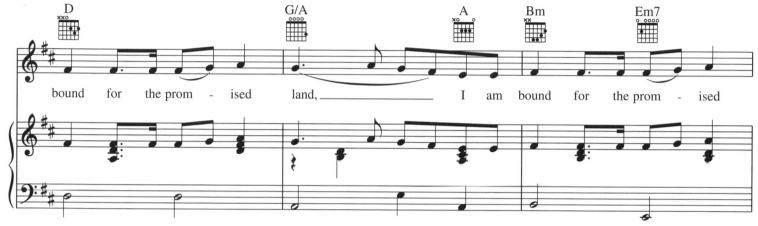

bound for the prom - ised land, _____ I am bound for the prom - ised

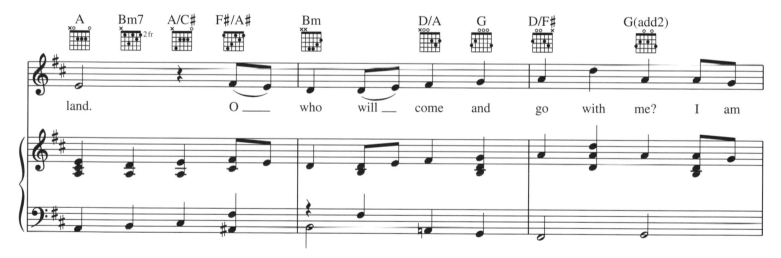

land. O __ who will __ come and go with me? I am

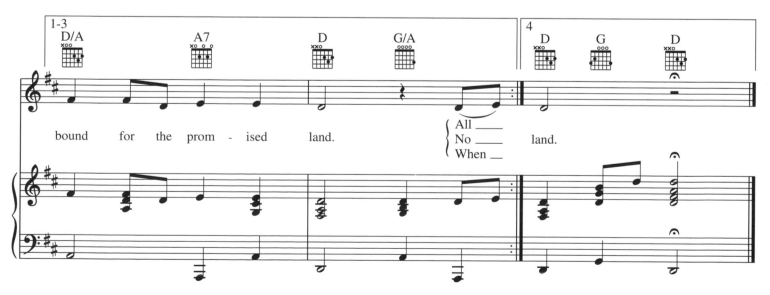

bound for the prom - ised land.

All __
No __ land.
When __

PANIS ANGELICUS
(O Lord Most Holy)

By CÉSAR FRANCK

coe - li-cus fi - gu - ris ter - mi - num. O res mi -

ra - bi-lis man - du - cat Do - mi-num, Pau - per,

pau - per, ser - vus et hu - mi - lis, Pau - per,

pau - per, ser - vus et hu - mi - lis.

ra - bi-lis, man - du-cat Do - mi-num Pau - per, _

O res mi - ra - bi-lis, man - du - cat Do - mi-num

pau - per, ser - vus et hu - mi - lis, Pau - per, _

Pau - per, _ ser - vus et hu - mi - lis, Pau - per, _

I,II unison

pau - per, ser - vus, _ ser - vus et hu - mi - lis.

decresc.

p

(There'll Be)
PEACE IN THE VALLEY
(For Me)

Words and Music by
THOMAS A. DORSEY

3. There the bear will be gentle, the wolf will be tame,
   And the lion will lay down by the lamb,
   The host from the wild will be led by a Child,
   I'll be changed from the creature I am.

4. No headaches or heartaches or misunderstands,
   No confusion or trouble won't be,
   No frowns to defile, just a long endless smile,
   There'll be peace and contentment for me.

PRECIOUS LORD, TAKE MY HAND
(Take My Hand, Precious Lord)

Words and Music by
THOMAS A. DORSEY

ROCK OF AGES

Words by AUGUSTUS M. TOPLADY
Altered by THOMAS COTTERILL
Music by THOMAS HASTINGS

TEARS ARE A LANGUAGE

Words and Music by
GORDON JENSEN

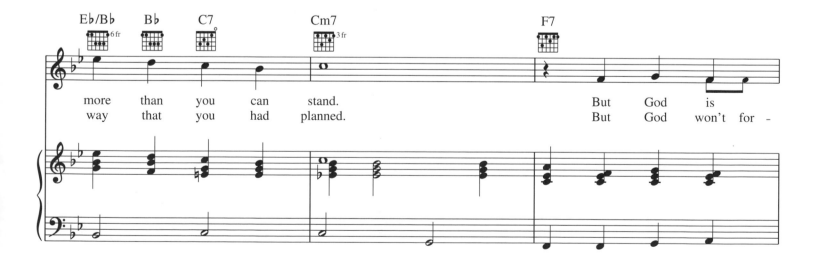

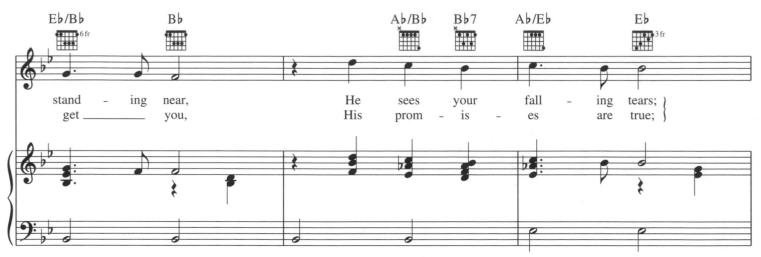

stand - ing near, He sees your fall - ing tears;
get _____ you, His prom - is - es are true;

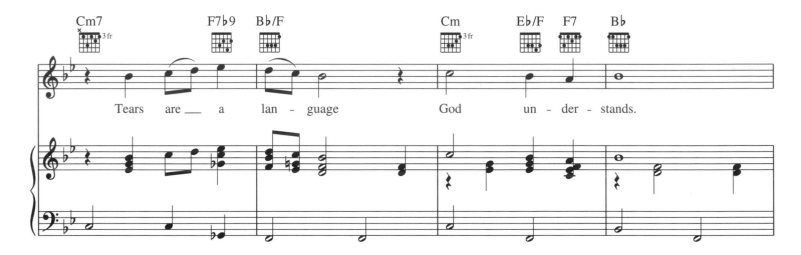

Tears are _ a lan - guage God un - der - stands.

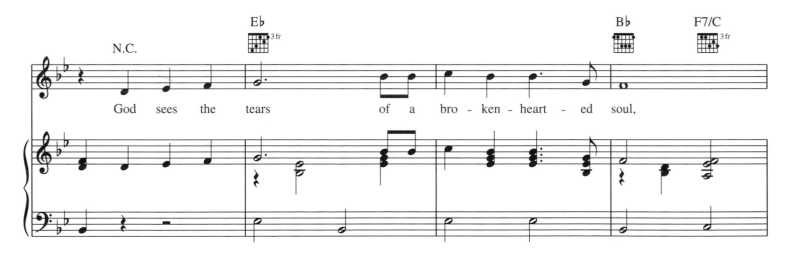

God sees the tears of a bro - ken - heart - ed soul,

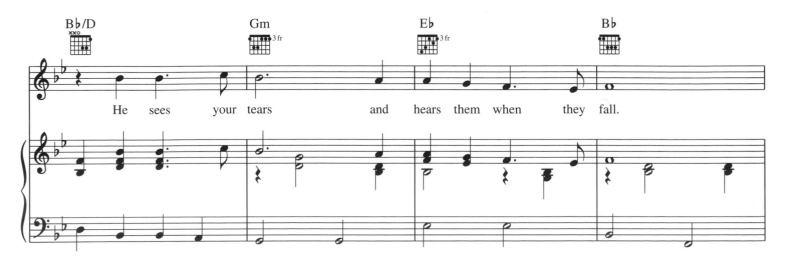

He sees your tears and hears them when they fall.

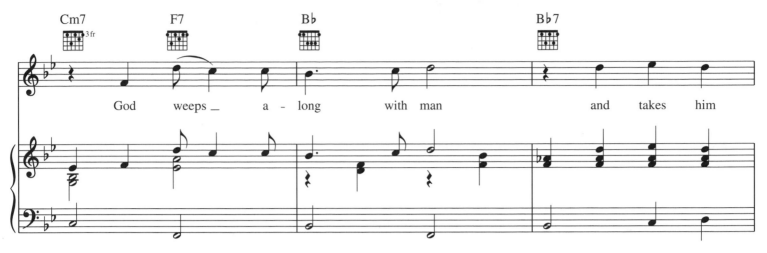

God weeps __ a - long with man and takes him

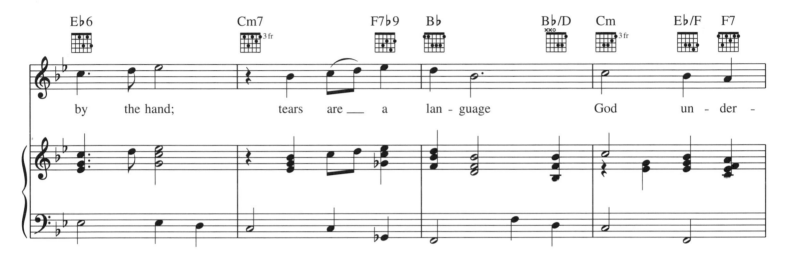

by the hand; tears are __ a lan - guage God un - der -

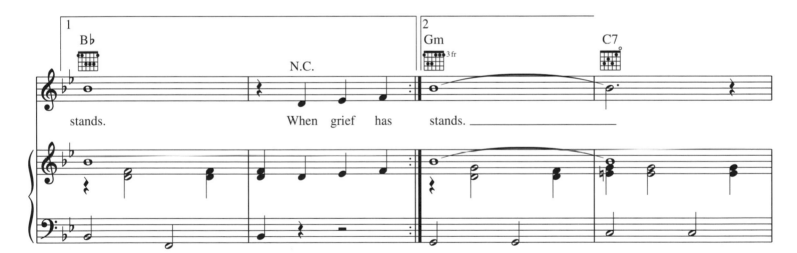

stands. When grief has stands. ___

God un - der - stands. ___

SWEET BY AND BY

Words by SANFORD FILLMORE BENNETT
Music by JOSEPH P. WEBSTER

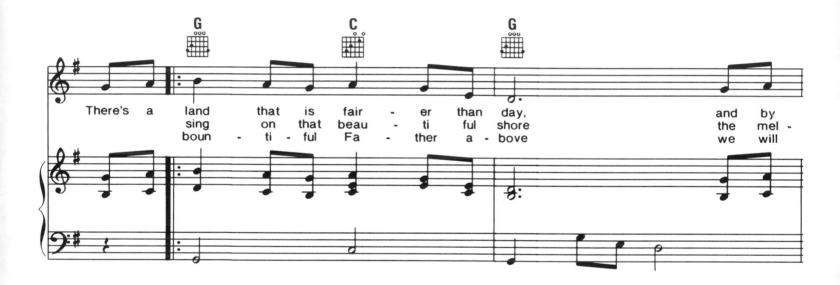

There's a land that is fair - er than day,
sing on that beau - ti - ful shore
boun - ti - ful Fa - ther a - bove

and by
we will

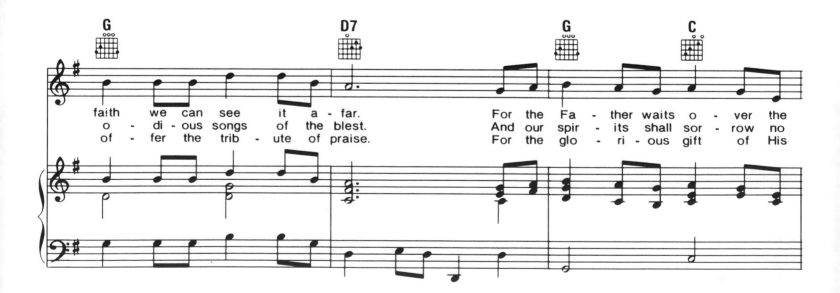

faith we can see it a - far.
o - di - ous songs of the blest.
of - fer the trib - ute of praise.

For the Fa - ther waits o - ver the
And our spir - its shall sor - row no
For the glo - ri - ous gift of His

SWING LOW, SWEET CHARIOT

Traditional Spiritual

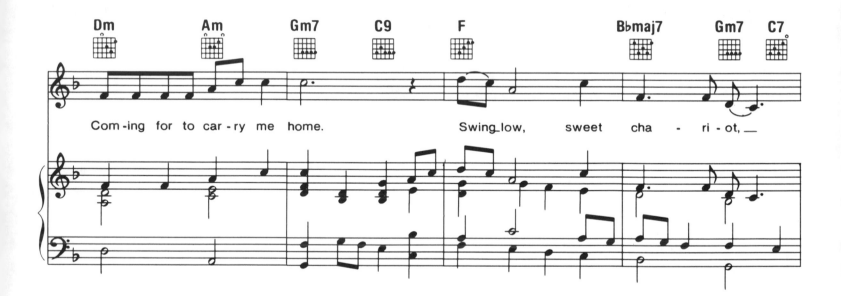

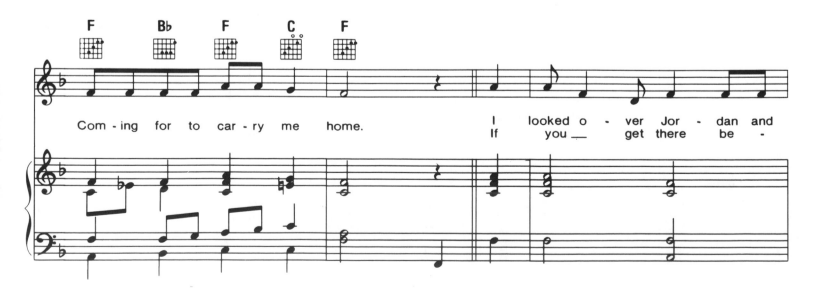

THEN SHALL THE RIGHTEOUS SHINE

from ELIJAH

By FELIX MENDELSSOHN

Andante sostenuto (♩ = 80)

Then, then ___ shall the right - eous shine forth as the
Dann wer - den die Ge - rech - ten leuch - ten, wie die

sun in their heav'n-ly Fa - ther's realm, shine forth as the
Son - ne in ih - res Va - ters Reich, *leuch - ten, wie die*

sun in their heav'n-ly Fa - ther's realm, then shall the right - eous shine forth in their
Son - ne in ih - res Va - ters Reich. *Dann wer-den die Ge - rech - ten, die Ge -*

flee   a - way,   shall   flee _____ a - way for - ev - er.
Seuf - *zen wird vor ih - nen flie - hen,* ____ *vor ih - nen flie - hen.*

Then,   then ____ shall   the right - eous shine   forth   as the sun   in their heav'n-ly
Dann   *wer - den die Ge-rech - ten leuch* - *ten, wie die Son* - *ne in ih - res*

Fa - ther's realm,   shine   forth,   shine   in their heav'n - ly Fa - ther's ___
Va - *ters Reich. Leuch* - *ten,*   *leuch* - *ten in ih - res Va - ters* ___

THE TWENTY-THIRD PSALM

By ALBERT H. MALOTTE

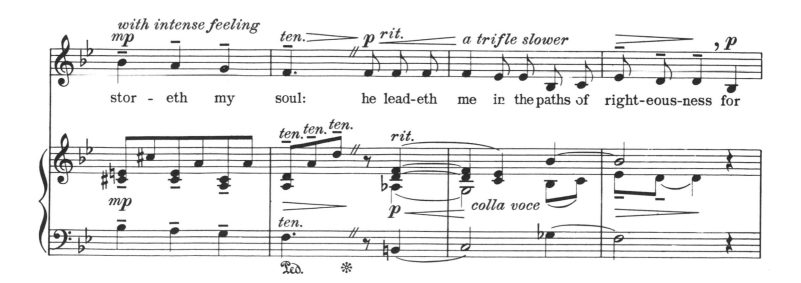

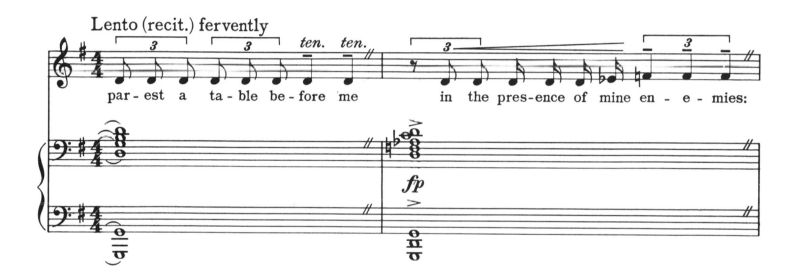

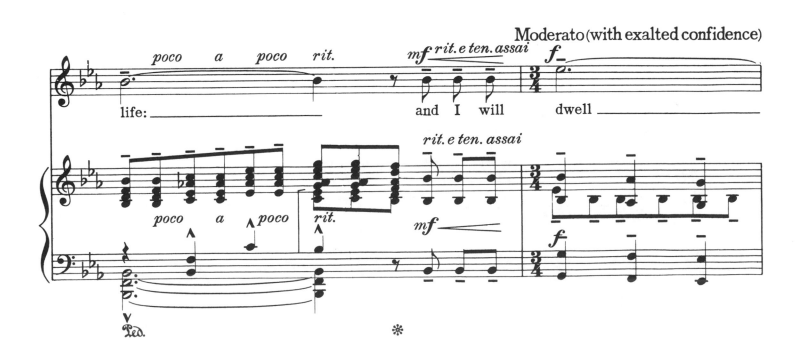

in the house of the Lord for

ev - - - er, and ev - - - er -

more.

WE'LL UNDERSTAND IT BETTER BY AND BY

Words and Music by
CHARLES A. TINDLEY

by. By and by, when the morn-ing comes All the saints of

God are gath-ered home, We'll tell the sto - ry how we've o - ver-come, For we'll

un - der-stand it bet - ter by and by. We are by.

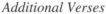

Additional Verses

2. We are often destitute of the things that life demands,
    Want of food and want of shelter, thirsty hills and barren lands,
    We are trusting in the Lord, and according to His word,
    We will understand it better by and by.
    Refrain

3. Trials dark on every hand, and we cannot understand,
    All the ways that God would lead us to that blessed Promised Land;
    But He guides us with His eye and we'll follow till we die,
    For we'll understand it better by and by.
    Refrain

4. Temptations, hidden snares often take us unawares,
    And our hearts are made to bleed for a thoughtless word or deed,
    And we wonder why the test when we try to do our best,
    But we'll understand it better by and by.
    Refrain

WHAT A FRIEND WE HAVE IN JESUS

Words by JOSEPH M. SCRIVEN
Music by CHARLES C. CONVERSE

Moderately

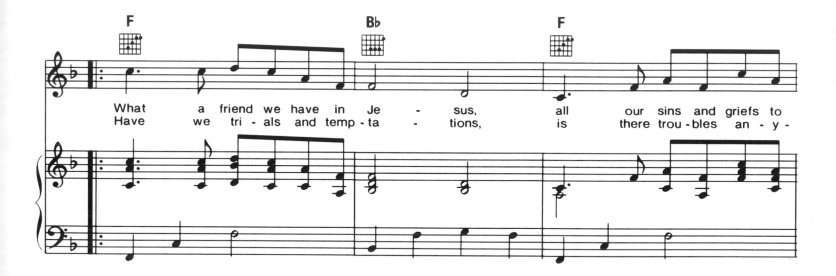

What a friend we have in Je - sus, all our sins and griefs to
Have we tri - als and temp - ta - tions, is there trou - bles an - y -

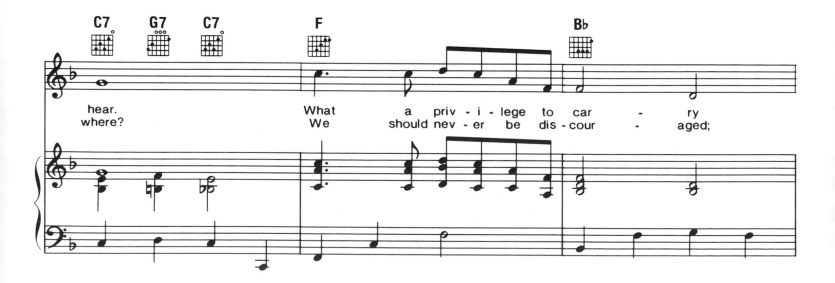

hear. What a priv - i - lege to car - ry
where? We should nev - er be dis - cour - aged;

3. Are we weak and heavy laden,
cumbered with a load of care?
Precious Savior still our refuge;
take it to the Lord in prayer.
Do thy friends despise, forsake thee?
Take it to the Lord in prayer.
In His arms He'll take and shield thee;
thou will find a solace there.

WHEN I LAY MY BURDEN DOWN

African-American Spiritual

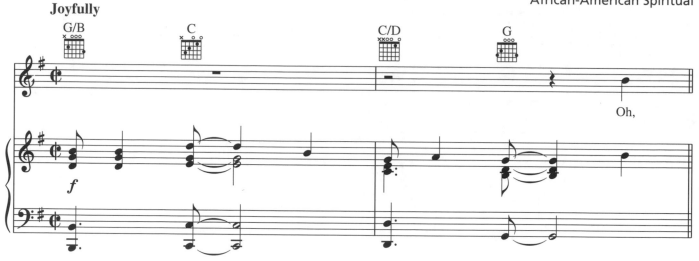

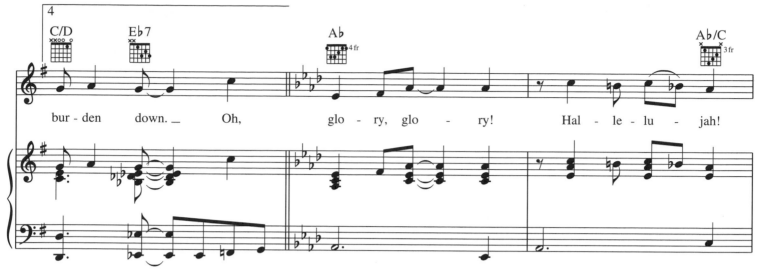

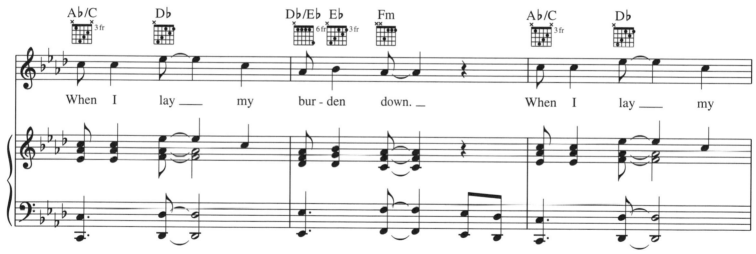

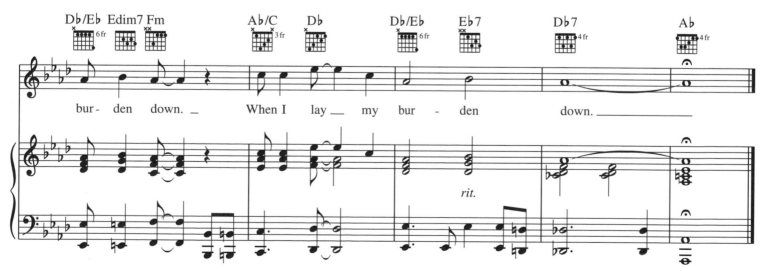

WHEN WE ALL GET TO HEAVEN

Words by ELIZA E. HEWITT
Music by EMILY D. WILSON

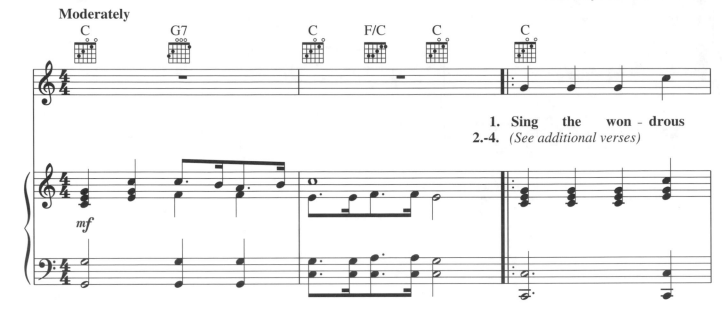

1. Sing the won-drous
2.-4. *(See additional verses)*

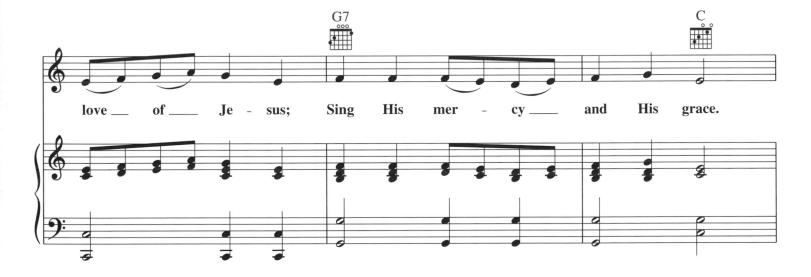

love ___ of ___ Je - sus; Sing His mer - cy ___ and His grace.

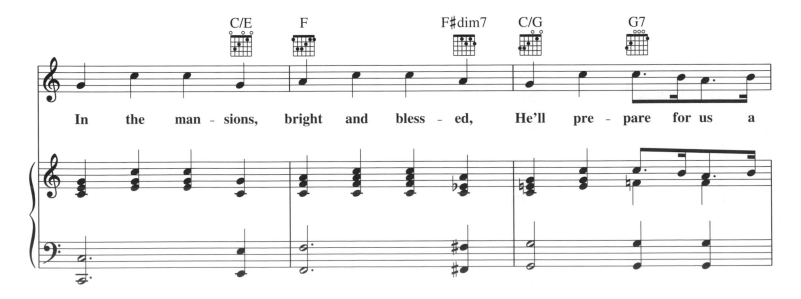

In the man - sions, bright and bless - ed, He'll pre - pare for us a

Additional Verses

2. While we walk the pilgrim pathway,
   Clouds will overspread the sky;
   But when trav'ling days are over,
   Not a shadow, not a sigh!
   Refrain

3. Let us then be true and faithful,
   Trusting, serving ev'ryday.
   Just one glimpse of Him in glory
   Will the toils of life repay.
   Refrain

4. Onward to the prize before us!
   Soon His beauty we'll behold.
   Soon the pearly gates will open;
   We shall tread the streets of gold.
   Refrain

YOU'LL NEVER WALK ALONE

from CAROUSEL

Lyrics by OSCAR HAMMERSTEIN II
Music by RICHARD RODGERS

Andantino molto cantabile

(with great warmth, like a hymn)

* alternate lyric: hold your head up high

The Finest Inspirational Music

Songbooks arranged for piano, voice, and guitar.

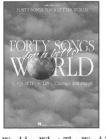

40 SONGS FOR A BETTER WORLD

40 songs with a message, including: All You Need Is Love • Bless The Beasts And Children • Colors Of The Wind • Everything Is Beautiful • He Ain't Heavy...He's My Brother • I Am Your Child • Love Can Build A Bridge • What A Wonderful World • What The World Needs Now Is Love • You've Got A Friend • and more.
00310096 ....$15.95

BEST GOSPEL SONGS EVER

80 of the best-loved Gospel songs of all time, including: Amazing Grace • At Calvary • Because He Lives • Behold the Lamb • Daddy Sang Bass • Get All Excited • His Eye Is on the Sparrow • I Saw the Light • I'd Rather Have Jesus • I'll Fly Away • Just a Little Talk With Jesus • Mansion Over the Hilltop • My Tribute • Precious Lord, Take My Hand • and more.
00310503 ....$19.95

CHRISTIAN CHILDREN'S SONGBOOK

Over 80 songs from Sunday School, including: Awesome God • The B-I-B-L-E • The Bible Tells Me So • Clap Your Hands • Day by Day • He's Got the Whole World in His Hands • I Am a C-H-R-I-S-T-I-A-N • I'm in the Lord's Army • If You're Happy (And You Know It) • Jesus Loves Me • Kum Ba Yah • Let There Be Peace on Earth • This Little Light of Mine • When the Saints Go Marching In • and more.
00310472 ....$19.95

CHRISTIAN WEDDING SONGBOOK

Over 30 contemporary Christian wedding favorites, including: Bonded Together • Butterfly Kisses • Commitment Song • Flesh of My Flesh • Go There with You • Household of Faith • How Beautiful • Love Will Be Our Home • Make Us One • Parent's Prayer (Let Go of Two) • This Is the Day (A Wedding Song) • and more.
00310681 ....$16.95

CONTEMPORARY CHRISTIAN VOCAL GROUP FAVORITES

15 songs, including: The Basics Of Life • A Few Good Men • The Great Divide • Undivided • and more.
00310019 ....$10.95

CONTEMPORARY CHRISTIAN WEDDING SONGBOOK

30 appropriate songs for weddings, including: Household Of Faith • Love In Any Language • Love Will Be Our Home • Parents' Prayer • This Is Love • Where There Is Love • and more.
00310022 ....$14.95

COUNTRY/GOSPEL U.S.A.

50 songs written for piano/guitar/four-part vocal. Highlights: An American Trilogy • Daddy Sang Bass • He Set Me Free • I Saw The Light • I'll Meet You In The Morning • Kum Ba Yah • Mansion Over The Hilltop • Love Lifted Me • Turn Your Radio On • When The Saints Go Marching In • many more.
00240139 ....$10.95

FAVORITE HYMNS

An outstanding collection of 71 all-time favorites, including: Abide With Me • Amazing Grace • Ave Maria • Bringing In The Sheaves • Christ The Lord Is Risen Today • Crown Him With Many Crowns • Faith Of Our Fathers • He's Got The Whole World In His Hands • In The Sweet By And By • Jesus Loves Me! • Just A Closer Walk With Thee • Kum Ba Yah • A Mighty Fortress Is Our God • Onward Christian Soldiers • Rock Of Ages • Swing Low, Sweet Chariot • Were You There? • and many more!
00490436 ....$12.95

GREAT HYMNS TREASURY

A comprehensive collection of 70 favorites: Close To Thee • Footsteps Of Jesus • Amazing Grace • At The Cross • Blessed Assurance • Blest Be The Tie That Binds • Church In The Wildwood • The Church's One Foundation • God Of Our Fathers • His Eye Is On The Sparrow • How Firm A Foundation • I Love To Tell The Story • In The Garden • It Is Well With My Soul • Just A Closer Walk With Thee • Just As I Am • Nearer My God, To Thee • Now That We All Our God • The Old Rugged Cross • The Lily Of The Valley • We're Marching To Zion • Were You There? • What A Friend We Have In Jesus • When I Survey The Wondrous Cross • and more.
00310167 ....$12.95

THE NEW YOUNG MESSIAH

Matching folio to the album featuring today's top contemporary Christian artists performing a modern rendition of Handel's *Messiah*. Features Sandi Patty, Steven Curtis Chapman, Larnelle Harris, and others.
00310006 ....$16.95

OUR GOD REIGNS

A collection of over 70 songs of praise and worship, including: El Shaddai • Find Us Faithful • His Eyes • Holy Ground • How Majestic Is Your Name • Proclaim The Glory Of The Lord • Sing Your Praise To The Lord • Thy Word • and more.
00311695 ....$17.95

SMOKY MOUNTAIN GOSPEL FAVORITES

37 favorites, including: Amazing Grace • At Calvary • At The Cross • Blessed Assurance • Church In The Wildwood• I Love To Tell The Story • In The Garden • In The Sweet By And By • The Old Rugged Cross • Rock Of Ages • Shall We Gather At The River • Softly And Tenderly • Tell It To Jesus • Wayfaring Stranger • We're Marching To Zion • What A Friend We Have In Jesus • When The Roll Is Called Up Yonder • When We All Get to Heaven • and more.
00310161 ....$8.95

ULTIMATE GOSPEL – 100 SONGS OF DEVOTION

Includes: El Shaddai • His Eye Is On The Sparrow • How Great Thou Art • Just A Closer Walk With Thee • Lead Me, Guide Me • (There'll Be) Peace In The Valley (For Me) • Precious Lord, Take My Hand • Wings Of A Dove • more.
00241009 ....$19.95

FOR MORE INFORMATION, SEE YOUR LOCAL MUSIC DEALER, OR WRITE TO:

HAL•LEONARD® CORPORATION
7777 W. BLUEMOUND RD. P.O. BOX 13819 MILWAUKEE, WI 53213

Visit us at www.halleonard.com for a complete listing of titles.

Prices, contents, and availability subject to change without notice. Some products may not be available outside the U.S.A.

1201